CH00933217

THE FUGITIVE

BY THOMAS DANIELL

Now he slept in the cheapest coffins, the ones nearest the port, beneath the quartz-halogen floods that lit the docks all night like vast stages; where you couldn't see the lights of Tokyo for the glare of the television sky, not even the towering hologram logo of the Fuji Electric Company, and Tokyo Bay was a black expanse where gulls wheeled above drifting shoals of white styrofoam. Behind the port lay the city, factory domes dominated by the vast cubes of corporate arcologies. Port and city were divided by a narrow borderland of older streets, an area with no official name. Night City, with Ninsei at its heart. By day, the bars down Ninsei were shuttered and featureless, the neon dead, the holograms inert, waiting, under the poisoned silver sky.

William Gibson, *Neuromancer,* 1984

From the beginning, Toyo Ito has had a plan, a theory, a vision. His extraordinary work as an architect is paralleled by his equally prolific work as an author. One of the most influential Japanese architects of his, or any, generation, Ito has always written in order to build and built in order to write. Even so, he has never treated his essays as self-absorbed, self-justifying design manifestos, but as opportunities to comment on wider, tangential issues. Literary and anecdotal in approach, he tells stories about his experiences with people, places and times. Ito is admittedly not a neutral observer, more of an editorial commentator prone to exaggeration, alternately seduced and repelled by his surroundings. The implication is

3

always that his architecture, for all its radical creativity, is somehow a considered personal response to a given situation. Comprising an ongoing attempt to elucidate his own thinking, Ito's writings have made permanent impressions on the thinking of his peers and the younger generation of architects in Japan, as well as in the wider architectural world. His essays from 1971 to 1988 were compiled into an anthology called *Kaze no henyōtai*, released in 1989 and then reissued ten years later with a companion volume of essays from 1988 to 1999 called *Tōsō suru architecture* (both titles contain multiple nuances and allusions, but they might be roughly translated as 'Transfiguration of the Wind' and 'Permeably Layered Architecture'). While most famous Japanese architects publish anthologies like this late in their careers, Ito's is modest compared with, for example, the 18-volume hardcover set of Kisho Kurokawa's writings published in 2006. Nonetheless, the pace of Ito's writing has only accelerated since the turn of the millennium. Each new design provides the opportunity for an essay, or series of essays – preliminary concepts, construction processes, post-occupancy evaluations – and each essay sets the stage for new designs.

Ito's first published essay, 'The Logic of Uselessness', appeared in 1971, the same year that he founded his office, URBOT ('urban robot'). Theoretical statement, practical manifesto, cultural diagnosis, science-fiction homage, satirical short story and implicit critique of his peers and predecessors, it set the tone for the 40 years of ceaselessly innovative architectural experiments that have followed. Perhaps the essay's most striking aspect is its attitude toward authorship. Ito writes about his new office as if he is an outside observer, anthropomorphising (but that's not quite right; perhaps 'animating') it as an autonomous entity, out of his control, not even of his creation: an agency with agency. He describes URBOT as having been spawned by 'the city' after two years of gestation and mute observation, a reference to the interlude between his departure from the office of Kiyonori Kikutake in 1969 and the official beginning of his own practice. The essay presents Ito's first three designs (URBOT-001, URBOT-002 and URBOT-003, the first already built, the other two destined to remain on paper) as if they are literally the offspring of the office. Yet rather than siblings, they are children of each other: not discrete designs, but three succeeding generations of evolution, each one an enigmatic aluminium shell that is smaller and more hermetic than its predecessor. Ito describes them as if he were an architectural botanist or entomologist, emphasising that evolution is not a process of progressive improvement but only constant recalibration in response to environmental pressures, and one that can go awry as positive feedback loops run out of control. Making an analogy with stag antlers that have gradually evolved from weapons into cumbersome symbols of their original purpose, he describes the tubes that project from URBOT-001 to bring in natural light as having, by UR-BOT-003, become so distended that they provide only the faintest illumination. His design argument – presented in the guise of disinterested observation – is that only overt dysfunctionality can have any impact in a society that has become so rationalised. Here, then, is the logic of uselessness, a parody of the obstinate pursuit of functionalism so pervasive in the architectural profession of the time. Yet URBOT was not presented as a polemical antithesis of the prevailing ideology, but rather as its ineradicable, repressed counterpart. Drawing on the same cultural heritage, gendered as male, described as a malformed 'bastard' with 'recessive heredity' (one imagines an innocuous, retarded nephew of the mechanical monsters in Japanese manga and movies), URBOT was a manifestation of the always present, rarely expressed aspects of the genome of modern architecture.

However vivid his imagery, Ito's rhetoric (like that of many Japanese writers) also conveys its meaning via implication and suggestion, and sometimes even omission. The written words cumulatively form a template around other, conspicuously absent, statements and intentions. There is, for example, no mention of the influence of

Japanese architecture, whether traditional or modern, in this first essay. According to Ito, the spark that brought URBOT to life was ignited by a mix of laconic Californian cool and eccentric English escapism, exemplified by Charles Moore's Sea Ranch and Archigram's Instant City respectively. Yet Ito's depiction of innumerable capsules clinging to every surface and infiltrating every crevice of the city, the wreckage of abandoned capsules lying amid the rubble on the ground below, is surely a crazed extrapolation of the visionary city proposals of his former employer Kikutake and other members of the metabolist group. The capsule-as-dwelling was a key theme in metabolism, best articulated by Kisho Kurokawa's 'Capsule Declaration' of 1969, in which he proposed a mobile 'cyborg architecture' that would supposedly suit contemporary lifestyles – compact, efficient living pods outfitted with the most advanced technologies. The emblematic realisation of these principles was Kurokawa's own Nakagin Capsule Tower, which was under construction in 1971, its stylised profile already a distinctive, radical addition to the Tokyo skyline. In tacit response, like a metabolist experiment that has escaped from the lab and turned feral, URBOT is described as evolving into an independent, mobile capsule that expels any trace of information technology from inside itself – a futile rejection of his, and architecture's, inescapable destiny, inefficiency presented as a valorisation of architectural space for its own sake.

A bizarre polemic to be sure, the essay was in large part a reaction to the four years Ito had spent working in Kikutake's office. Ito's growing sense of doubt and disillusionment during that time was not due to the buildings, which he continued to deeply admire, but the methodology. The supposedly logical design processes that had initially attracted Ito to Kikutake were revealed as a sham, maintained for external publicity but abandoned within the office whenever expedient. Ito had quit (against Kikutake's wishes), intending to further his education but prevented from doing so by the widespread student rioting that shut down Japan's universities at the end of the 1960s. Instead, he began work on his first solo commission, URBOT-001, otherwise known as the Aluminium House. Ito had by then come under the influence of two slightly older architects who were to become the key theorists of their generation: Arata Isozaki, an erstwhile associate of the metabolists whose contributions to the movement were fraught with implicit criticism of its ambitions, and the charismatic fringe-figure Kazuo Shinohara, an outspoken opponent of metabolist technophilia and megalomania, known for his iconoclastic house projects and aphoristic theoretical manifestos. Politically active, artistically aware and historically literate, Isozaki has adeptly kept pace with the temper of the times, constantly adjusting his approach and audience. Shinohara, too, changed course several times across his career, but always within the self-imposed limits of his own hermetic discourse. Ito was deeply influenced by Shinohara's essays from the late 1960s and early 1970s, wherein he insisted that architects simply turn their backs on the city and focus on the creation of personal, miniature utopias, a stance that Isozaki was then tending toward. But if Ito admired the content, he was surely also inspired by the form in which it was being presented: the architect as writer, as public intellectual, a perceptive and severe critic of the existing order who could present both diagnoses and remedies through words as much as buildings – and who could achieve wide popular appeal precisely through a pretence of indifference toward popular appeal.

The end of Japan's postwar period of visionary urban projects had been signalled, ironically, by their partial realisation at the phenomenally ambitious 1970 Osaka Expo. The planning of the Expo was dominated by the metabolist group under the direction of architect Kenzo Tange and urbanist Uzo Nishiyama, who set the theme of a 'model core of a future city'. Isozaki and Kurokawa were key contributors, and Ito himself had been deeply immersed in the design as Kikutake's staff representative at the weekly project meetings. Intended to represent the promise of emancipated, technology-enabled urban lifestyles, the Expo was widely seen as having only highlighted the blighted environmental conditions under which most Japanese were then living. The cities were incoherent, ugly palimpsests of pre-modern towns, wartime devastation, hastily built new housing and brutally implanted infrastructure. The countryside was being steadily and thoughtlessly polluted in tragic counter-point to the industrialisation, urbanisation and modernisa-tion that had so rapidly brought Japan from physical and psychological ruin to First World levels of wealth. During the 1950s and 60s provincial governments had tried to attract industrial investment (mining, chemical production, wood pulp treatment) to rural areas, resulting in a series of notorious ecological disasters that contaminated traditional fishing and farming communities with industrial waste and caused outbreaks of birth defects and incurable diseases. With the wider population content in their rising prosperity, protests were initially suppressed or ignored, but media coverage and successful compensation claims finally forced the Japanese government to act: 1971 was also the year that an Environmental Agency was established in order to enforce new strict pollution laws.

Ito was thus part of a generation that could no longer see technology as Japan's unproblematic salvation from wartime destruction, but as potentially destructive itself. His architectural response to environmental pollution (light and sound as much as air and earth) is adumbrated in the 1976 essay 'White Ring', which describes the design of White U, the house that he considers to be the real start of his solo career. While its striking physical form and conceptual isolation from the city clearly reflect the influence of Shinohara, Ito was not, of course, the only architect of the time to have opted to overtly seal his houses against what was generally regarded as an unsalvageable context. Yet while many of the fortress-like houses built by others – the blank concrete facade of Tadao Ando's Row House in Sumiyoshi, also completed in 1976, was the iconic image for Japanese residential architecture of the period – were, metaphorically speaking, bubbles of pure air inflated within a contaminated atmosphere, Ito described his architecture as containers for samples of that same atmosphere, their interior spaces conceived as fields excised from the ambient light of the city. In the 1977 essay 'Signs of Light' Ito quotes Le Corbusier's canonical definition of architecture as the 'play of masses brought together in light' while redefining the qualities of the light itself. He describes Tokyo's atmosphere as a dull haze without real highlights or shadows, a combination of innumerable artificial sources and tepid sunlight filtered through permanent smog. This wasn't a unique observation. Among his contemporaries, Ando was saying much the same thing, but where Ando saw a problem to be overcome, Ito saw a condition to be optimised. The surfaces, orifices and objects that comprise White U are literally and conceptually bleached: painted pure white and detached from practical function, described as compositional 'morphemes' for the manipulation of lighting effects and the creation of a vague sense of spatial turbulence throughout a serene, introverted interior. Whether flat, stepping or gently curved, the surfaces appear smooth, insubstantial, unarticulated – architecture without relief, so to speak. Sequestered in the centre of the house was a bleak 'garden', an expanse of black soil that unavoidably evoked the scorched earth left by the firestorms that devastated Tokyo in the closing months of the war.

This consummate and, needless to say, exceptionally beautiful implementation of principles drawn from Shinohara also contained the first hints of Ito's impending shift away. By the late 1970s Ito was considered to be a key figure in an unofficial 'Shinohara School' of contemporary Japanese architecture, for which Shinohara himself was busy claiming a range of members that extended far beyond his actual students, often without their knowledge or consent. Yet in the first published mention of the Shinohara School (a 1979 magazine feature that included profiles of Shinohara, Ito, Kazunari Sakamato and Itsuko Hasegawa) Ito is already described as a 'failed student', an adept who had diverged from, if not transcended, the master. In 1979 URBOT vanished; Ito renamed his office Toyo Ito & Associates. He also left the orbit of Shinohara, even temporarily forming an 'anti-Shinohara' group with colleagues such as critic Koji Taki. Avoiding explicit references to architectural precedent in his writing of the 1980s, Ito's focus turned toward the city, encompassing a range of intellectual and sensual, even erotic – sight, sound, smell, touch – interpretations of the contemporary urban experience. The essay 'Silver Hut' introduces the period of work that began in 1984 with the completion of Ito's own house, also called Silver Hut, yet instead of describing the architecture, Ito expresses his desire to create images of futuristic cities, inspired by science-fiction movies (or more accurately, by his disappointment with the set designs of most science-fiction movies of the period). Here is an unashamed admission of Ito's proto-*otaku* tendencies. Enthusiasm for the liberating fantasies of futuristic manga and movies suffuses his work, like the toy-laden shelves of an obsessive science-fiction fan – from the heavy metal articulations of robots to the ephemeral cinematic effects of light and motion, along with a perverse pleasure in the dystopian gloom latent within every vision of a gleaming technological utopia. We can imagine Ito growing up in the high-tech favela, the neon-lit squalor of Tokyo after the war. The traumas of firebombing, defeat and occupation were being sublimated by artists (the 'anti-art' and 'non-art' movements, the Gutai Art Association and Butoh Dance Group). The massive reconstruction efforts were seen as an opportunity for Japan to implement future cities of unprecedented technological sophistication and social mobility – topics debated by serious intellectuals and depicted in popular culture. Japanese society was permeated by an avant-garde sensibility, a dissatisfaction with the present and a sense of urgency and optimism with regard to the future. The seeds of Ito's desire to create pristine, weightless spaces for immaculately garbed, perfectly formed androids, as well as his fascination with dynamic, incoherent urban environments, may be found here.

Silver Hut was completed at the beginning of the most extreme period of Japan's postwar economic growth, the so-called 'bubble'. For Ito, the superficiality of the lifestyles being engendered by Japan's incredible new wealth was matched by the superficiality of its urban environment. The commercial districts of Tokyo were being demolished and rebuilt at an astonishing rate. New buildings were intended from the outset as temporary fashion statements, their electronic signage dominating their physical substance. Ito wanted to distil the city's ever-intensifying nervous energy into a visual rhetoric for architectural design. Rather than the creation of iconic objects anchored within an amorphous, volatile context, his new ambition was to develop an iconography of the context itself – even, perhaps, to define a new vernacular for contemporary Tokyo. Where Isozaki's architecture, for example, aspired to some kind of intellectualised ideal, Ito's was conceived as a description of the actual world he saw around him. No longer interested in precious, opaque volumes penetrated by tubes and slots that bring in controlled shafts or washes of exterior light, Ito began to explore the poetic potentials of new materials – diaphanous artificial fabrics, transparent acrylic sheets, flexible steel meshes, perforated aluminium panels – in order to contrive entire buildings as porous, translucent shells that appear to be condensed from the ambient light itself. Prefigured by the lifestyles of the comparatively wealthy, as yet unmarried, young women of Tokyo, endlessly pursuing fashion and sensation yet unable to escape their ennui, the hypothetical inhabitant of this architecture was the urban 'nomad', a fugitive individual in a world of fugitive phenomena.

Ito's writing of this period was not an unqualified celebration of the unstable, artificial, 'simulated' qualities of lifestyles in bubble-era Tokyo. If the notion of the urban nomad seems to echo Kurokawa's earlier celebration of the emergence of *homo movens* ('mobile man'), Ito is scathing about the environment from which the urban nomad emerges, then perpetuates and exacerbates. In the 1988 essay 'What is the Reality of Architecture in a Futuristic

City?' Ito suggested that the citizens of Tokyo were unwittingly becoming 'android-like', then in the seminal 1991 essay 'Architecture for the Simulated City', he asserts that contemporary urban life is depriving them of the ability to even discriminate between fake and real. Even so, he refuses to make a quixotic retreat into an archaic and ostensibly 'authentic' treatment of architectural materials and spaces. Ito launched himself into the emerging urban conditions, encapsulating his objectives in the phrase 'design of atmosphere': the invention of a type of architecture that might register and visualise in real time all the invisible qualities of its surroundings. While this included variations in temperatures, breezes, odours, sounds – properties inseparable from their physical substrate – Ito also contended that the city's atmosphere is permeated with insubstantial flows of information, which we may subconsciously perceive and architecture should consciously represent.

The idea that Japanese urban spaces are somehow shrouded in a flickering electronic haze had first appeared in Isozaki's writings of the early 1960s, in which he makes an analogy between the information flows generated by new media and the immanent *hi* (spirit) of Shinto cosmology. If Isozaki is rigorous in his historiography, he is all too often mystical in his use of historical concepts. Isozaki's invocation of *hi* may have been intended as an evocative cultural curiosity, but Ito's description of an invisible parallel world permeating the tangible one was not merely metaphorical. He intended the notion of information to be understood in the strictly materialist sense of electromagnetic fields: visible light, video transmissions, radio waves and so on. While our increasingly ubiquitous wireless communication networks might be thoughtlessly envisaged as cartoon lightning bolts leaping between mobile phones or personal computers, the reality is a kind of informational ether: an unthinkably complex interference pattern of overlapping spherical ripples propagating from innumerable sources at the speed of light. Ito's architecture of the 1980s, exemplified by the Tower of Winds in Yokohama, was an attempt to represent all of these flows poetically. Knowingly or not, Ito recalls the Tower of Winds as described by Vitruvius – an octagonal form symbolising the direction of the 'eight winds', incorporating a wind vane, sundial and water clock – but whereas Vitruvius's tower was to be a focal point for laying out a new city, Ito's coalesces from an existing one. Built form is here conceived as a filter or sensor that somehow intercepts the flux of information, slowing and condensing it, making it momentarily perceptible, even palpable: architecture that flickers and buzzes like faulty neon, that is washed with intermittent static like a weak video signal. His metaphor is architecture as a kind of 'spray' that coats and thereby reveals the spectral outlines of the informational field, like water droplets modelling air turbulence or metal filings tracing a magnetic field. Ito again implies that he is not an author but an instrument, a medium – not imposing designs on the world, but manifesting its existing, unseen patterns.

Largely a reaction to Japan's phenomenal economic strength and the concomitant destabilising effects on architectural and urban form, Ito's diagnosis of built substance attenuating into transient imagery culminated in his contribution to the exhibition 'Visions of Japan' at London's Victoria & Albert Museum (17 September 1991 – 5 January 1992). Ironically, this was held just as Japan's economic strength was vanishing: its bubble burst at the beginning of the 1990s. Not a sudden collapse, it was an erratic, flatulent deflation that took years. The relative sobriety of the ensuing decade saw a second significant shift in Ito's interests, from the contemporary urban environment to the embodied experience of its inhabitants. Refusing the nostalgic notion of some sort of 'natural' human physiological and perceptual core to which architecture should always respond, Ito instead asserted that the human body must adapt to its artificial habitat (or has already done so). In the 1997 essay 'Tarzans in the Media Forest' he introduced one of his most radical concepts, that of the 'virtual body': not a replacement

for flesh and blood but a parallel, phantom existence,
a doppelganger embedded in the electronic realm, a
newly liberated noble savage roaming the fluid world
of information. The role of architecture, then, was to
act as an intermediary between the physical body and the
virtual body, as exemplified by Ito's design for the Sendai
Mediatheque – a pivotal project in the evolution of his
own work and, indeed, the discipline of architecture as
a whole.

Initially designed in 1995 and finally completed in
2001, the intervening years of public debates over the
Mediatheque and its gruelling construction process
triggered a further, decisive shift in Ito's theoretical focus.
Listening to the protests of the local citizens and witnessing
the infernal sights and sounds on site caused him to
fundamentally re-evaluate the stance he had developed
over the preceding decades. Ito was no stranger to building
sites – indeed, in 'White Ring' he says that the inspiration
for the lighting design of White U came from observing the
temporary lights used by the builders – but as his work
increased in scale and ambition, it was clear that the closer
he came to achieving the ethereal, cerebral spaces of a
'virtual' architecture, the longer and harsher were his
collisions with the brute, visceral materiality of
construction. To the extent that it had been inspired by
science-fiction movies, his architecture was less about
modelling futuristic stage sets than implementing the
types of perceptual effects – transience, luminescence,
instantaneity, insubstantiality – that are specific to cinema.
The realisation of the Mediatheque was a conclusive
demonstration that he was undertaking a Sisyphean task:
the lighter he was able to float, the heavier the weight
dragging him back down. In a retroactive repudiation
of his own early intuitions, Ito stopped attempting to
escape the limitations of physical architecture, and instead
embraced them. Unhappily aware of the extent of his
influence on the pallid, skeletal work of younger Japanese
architects (raising his concerns in 1998's 'Shedding the
Modern Body Image' and again in 2002's 'Ichiro-like

Architects'), in the first decade of the new millennium Ito's thought and work turned toward weight, opacity, texture and, above all, nature. Architecture was no longer to be designed for the virtual body but for the primitive body, and built form was to acknowledge its origins in the natural, material world.

Not – at least, not solely – a visual mimicry of natural forms, this was rather an attempt to emulate natural processes through architecture: in the expressive qualities of structures and spaces and in their integration with wider flows of energy and matter through permeable outer membranes. Nor was this a retreat from technology. Particularly in the work undertaken together with leading structural engineers Mutsuro Sasaki (an ongoing collaboration that began with the mediatheque) and Cecil Balmond, Ito has used the computer as a gateway to a fluid world of emergent shapes that mimic the evolution and growth of natural structures. Here, Ito comes full circle with URBOT, again implying that he is no more than an observer of a self-organising architecture out of his control – and again, this is a ruse. Ito is not ceding decisions about architectural form to parametric software, sitting entranced by intricate, pointless patterns unfurling on a computer monitor or emerging from a CNC mill. While the computer allows embryonic design concepts to be iteratively evolved toward optimal functional and structural configurations within the field of forces at work – internal ergonomic and programmatic demands, external legal and climatic pressures – this takes place under Ito's direct supervision and input, departing as little as possible from his intended spatial and aesthetic effects.

The four distinct stages of Ito's theoretical develop-ment so far (robot, city, body, nature) almost exactly coincide with his four decades of practice. It is a trajectory that suggests a telescoped reversal of the history of human civilisation, propelled toward its origins by the most advanced technologies. Programmatically, there is an almost classical sequence from his 'primitive' Silver Hut through the iconic Tower of Winds to the Sendai Mediatheque as agora or forum, the users shifting from isolated individuals to freely interacting collectives. Thematically, there is a progressive zoom in from the planetary city to the cellular level of organic life. We might tentatively predict that the fifth phase of Ito's theoretical concepts will reflect a state prior to the emergence of life itself: the formation of autocatalytic molecular structures in the primeval soup of our planet's prebiotic oceans. Indeed, something similar is already hinted at in the crystalline, modular forms of Ito's recent designs.

Throughout his writings, Ito presents himself with an admirable, if odd humility, insisting that he is merely observing, following, tracing, visualising or manifesting forces already at work (he is also famous for disingenuously insisting that it is his staff who produce the ideas and his structural engineers who produce the forms). This affected and affecting self-effacement is, perhaps, no more than a strategy that allows him to pursue the most extreme architectural experiments without triggering the kind of public backlash against perceived megalomania that makes so many architects their own worst enemy. He makes it all seem natural, even inevitable.

Making Ito's essays available in English is an ongoing, collective task occurring piecemeal around the world. The translations now available form only a small fraction of his steadily increasing body of writing, and no doubt have been selected as much for their literary interest as for their theoretical significance. Even if they manage to suggest the breadth of Ito's thought, it is, of course, impossible to fully convey the subtleties of his voice. Often conversational and colloquial in tone, Ito's essays tend to recall the work of contemporary novelists rather than architectural theorists. He evokes the deadpan surrealism of Haruki Murakami's postmodern detective stories, for example, or the persistent attention to everyday phenomena found in novels such as Banana Yoshimoto's *Kitchen*. While Ito has moments of hyperbole, he avoids the manifesto-like assertions of Kurokawa and the obscure, archaic *kanji* favoured by Isozaki. His most extreme speculations are presented without pretention, characterised by a restrained wit and an understated, yet undeniable, love of the world in which he finds himself.

Unlike translating between European languages, in which precise analogues for individual words may be found and differences in grammatical structure may be almost mechanically resolved, translating Japanese into English is never without irreducible ambiguities. Direct translations of all but the simplest Japanese sentences will usually be unintelligible, but overly mellifluous translations must be regarded as suspect – the effect of rhetorical liberties that may have obscured original intents. In the process of deciphering the literal meaning, nudging the result into grammatically correct English and then polishing it smooth, the translator is forced to make judgement calls on the precision of the assertions and the preservation of the metaphors. While any author may sometimes intend to be obscure or allusive, there is a licence for ambiguous assertion in non-fiction writing in Japan that is appreciated and indulged far more than in the West, and may be found at a surprisingly scholarly level. In many cases the cultural background of Japanese readers will allow them to be automatically cued by the choices between almost synonymous *kanji* characters, which may subtly evoke archaism, exoticism, religiosity, canonic literary works and so on. At best, the translator can attempt to structure each sentence to lean toward a similar range of possible interpretations, if only by analogy. Much of the poetry of Ito's prose is unavoidably lost, but the mood is retained.

Of course, the written discourse of any architect is usually less a rigorous argument than it is a special pleading for a particular aesthetic agenda. A theory is never disinterested, always a justification for a style, a way to hone and crystallise one's intuitions about form and space. Ito incessantly reacts to the times and places he passes through, with the sensibility of a novelist who occasionally veers into magical realism or new journalism. Telling stories that explain, enable, inspire or validate his architectural experiments, he often absents himself from the picture, or depicts himself as a passive observer of events. In this sense, 'Toyo Ito' can be understood as that favourite trope of modernist literature, the unreliable narrator. Ito invites us to share in the way he sees the world, the texts and buildings alike providing clues to his ever-changing moods. Through them, we may temporarily, sympathetically inhabit Toyo Ito's mind and body, tracing his evolving narrative of the last four decades as he enters a fifth, always one step ahead of his pursuers.

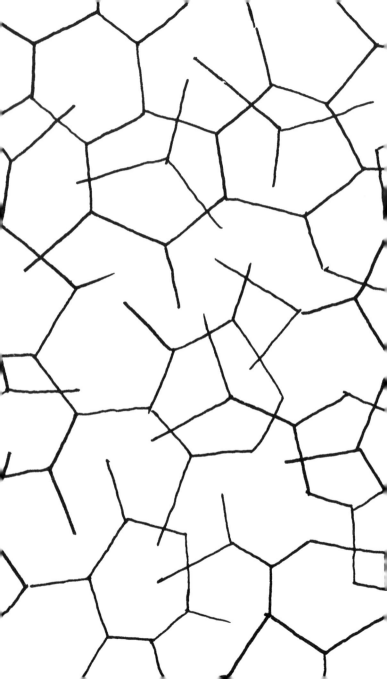

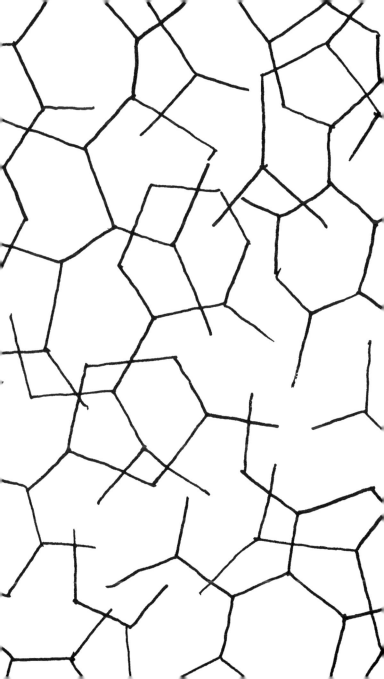

THE LOGIC OF USELESSNESS
(1971)

In the summer of 1971, the bastard architecture URBOT was spawned by a city suffused with a sense of listlessness arising from its faith in, and resignation to dominance by, technology. Its full name is URBAN ROBOT.

Over a period of two years, URBOT had quietly observed the movements of society. In the same way that insects flitting about in the air first spend long larval periods underground, awaiting their turn, he held his breath and observed every detail of the movements around him. The urban spaces in his surroundings were undergoing great transformations. Multistorey buildings made of huge steel frames were taking shape, their outer surfaces clad with white, scale-like, precast concrete units, while endless dreary plazas and parks were being created, based on a blind faith that salvation would be assured by chanting 'community, community' like a mantra.

From what URBOT could gather, if developments continued to optimistically extend in the same direction, Tokyo's fate would be to take on the form of a 'mechanistoria': a city endowed with vast, extensive management mechanisms under the perfect control of a 'town brain' comprising large-scale computers and robots equipped with all manner of information devices.

There, within dwelling capsules that acted as information terminals, each individual person would have sex, eat and sleep.

If URBOT were able to function as an elite next-generation architecture – one of a group of competent urban robots, acting as a terminal within an individual dwelling as well as serving as a community information portal – this would result in an integrated human–machine system.

Having been implemented by manufacturing mechanisms that place absolute confidence in technology, he would undoubtedly be accepted by society.

However, while sensing the appeal of having powerful information devices installed within himself, URBOT was hesitant. It was similar to the desire to avoid becoming a businessman in a major corporation. His hesitancy was not an ideological confusion arising from being inserted in an enormous administrative apparatus, but was provoked by the non-mechanical, non-technological, irrational emotions that roiled within him.

In his eyes, the image of a 'mechanistoria' informational city was nothing more than the collective illusion of a homogeneous world, whereas he could only feel reality in those spaces that transmitted the warmth of human breath and corporeality.

One of Stanislaw Lem's novels, titled *The Invincible*, deals with natural selection among autonomous, self-replicating machines. A spaceship alights on the science-fiction setting of the planet Regis III to discover that every living thing has been annihilated and the planet has been occupied by autonomous machines that are able to reproduce, causing natural selection to occur among them. As a result, there are just two remaining types of autonomous machines now locked in a battle for survival. The first has a shape like an extremely small insect, and during combat they merge into an enormous mass that resembles a dark cloud spilling across the sky, disabling their opponents' information-exchange mechanisms. The second is an immobile machine that absorbs solar energy through an unusual organ like a triangular metallic plate, and possesses the reproductive power of a huge colony, like a metal forest. Ultimately, the second type loses the struggle for existence and becomes a vast ruin, like a metallic city, and a grand battle unfolds between the crew of the spaceship and the surviving machines – though with no chance of success for the humans. Some parallels could be drawn between the imagery of Lem's science-fiction world and the incredible ongoing expansion of the bizarre urban future that is named Tokyo. Comprising a countless number of uniform cuboid cells, it gives the impression of an eternal battle between vertically extending steel-framed skyscrapers and low-rise concrete dwellings covering the ground surface. This battle ends with the victory of the skyscrapers, equipped with advanced control mechanisms and innumerable capsules clinging to their scattered, soaring steel frames, like an abundant grape harvest spilling from overflowing shelves. Below is a concrete desert of crumbling white sand endlessly stirred by a freezing wind, the remnants of abandoned capsules buried in the sand like rotting fruit. While people contort their bodies within the cramped capsules, encircled by all manner of information terminals, peals of eerie vibrato laughter may be heard between the thickets of metal trees.

The unhappiness arising from URBOT's hesitation to embed information terminals within his body originates in the misapprehension of a genealogy of ideas that could also be described as his parents.

The architectural world of the 1970s was in a chaotic state – blending, resisting and adapting theories about information cities, capsules, community, paranoia, pop architecture, design surveys, systems, customs, utopias, vernacularism and so on. Mediated by the concept of spatial control, this situation was exemplified, for instance, by the ingenious coordination of the conventional image of the informational city and the psychedelic acid-trip world depicted in Tom Wolfe's *The Electric Kool-Aid Acid Test*, or by the fantastical utopias humorously presented in Archigram's projects for an Instant City and a Plug-in City, but debates about their relevance to the functionalist theories of standardisation, industrialisation and capsulisation in the housing industry only provoked laughter and irritation.

Tracing the threads of this complex entanglement, we arrive at two antithetical genealogies that greatly influenced the thinking of URBOT. One is the stream of Californian vernacular architecture exemplified by Charles W Moore and Joseph Esherick, the other is the stream of utopias in the work of Archigram and Superstudio.

In the dry climate of the West Coast evoked by *Easy Rider* and *Vanishing Point*, a stream of vernacular architecture – developed from the combination of redwood siding and monopitch roofs in the traditional shingle style – made its entrance in the form of a group of weekend houses called Sea Ranch, in which guileless, fresh spaces were created by the addition of the pop sensibility of supergraphics.

With architecture now reduced to manufacturing mechanisms and technologies, our sense of alienation intensifying as reality rapidly slips away, Sea Ranch's crystallisation of miniature structures made from familiar materials and techniques, such as wooden wall siding and supergraphics, was very attractive to URBOT.

On the other hand, those cool worlds delineated by Archigram and Superstudio – toying with utopianism and technology, displaying an utter lack of interest in connecting with theories of industrialisation in line with functionalism – still retained their appeal.

The two major streams from which URBOT gained life – California vernacularism and technological utopianism – share a desire to criticise the dominance of technological civilisation. But apart from this, their intentions and methods are oriented in completely opposite directions. Whereas the former pursues connections with region and climate, and tries to re-establish contact with an untouched nature, the latter comprises science fiction-style depictions of the paradoxical utopias that emerge from an exacerbation of the information and materials with which modern society is saturated.

It is not especially surprising that the attempt to abruptly superimpose these two conflicting motives resulted in the birth of URBOT, a malformed child with recessive heredity. Even in a world brimming with contradictions, such as returning to nature while worshipping technology, perhaps such a thing is possible in a city as anarchic as Tokyo. In any case, with the loss of his most important control function, URBOT became a useless member of society. Yet he wondered if the fact of his uselessness might allow him to occupy a unique position in society. In contemporary society, puzzlement at his baffling uselessness – a dysfunction explained as arising from his recessive heredity – might lead the busy people that inhabit, or visit, URBOT to ponder, become annoyed, then destroy and restructure him as something functional. This value arising from uselessness is filled with contradictions, but on account of its very illogicality, he thought that he had a meaningful existence within a rationally constructed society.

Inevitably, giving meaning to the existence of URBOT based upon this logic of uselessness gave rise to some particular contradictions.

Firstly, while URBOT advocates the negation of real conditions without leading to a simplistic focus on utopia, he wants his presence to manifest as a tangible shape in the real world. As I have already mentioned, he cannot avoid thinking about the realisation of utopia, even if it might suddenly lose its radiance, but rather than parting with reality by racing toward utopian idealism and coolly laughing at the transparent logic of reality, he thinks that architecture's essential nature lies precisely in savouring the absurdity of real life for an individual human being. Consequently, while URBOT possesses an endless yearning for the opposed directions of past and future inherited from each of his parents, whichever way he leans, he can never avoid looking directly at reality itself.

Secondly, while URBOT senses the unbearable sterility of the metropolitan environment exemplified by Tokyo, the fact is that he could not escape the environment of the city and survive. Taken to the extreme, placing one's body in a location with the greatest sense of contemporary alienation – temporal as well as spatial – allows this sensation of alienation to be directly expressed.

So however frivolous URBOT's selective sensitivity to his era may seem, the feelings that typify an era must be adhered to, and materials must also be chosen based upon these feelings.

In URBOT's interactions with reality, his appearance has been gradually distorted. Essentially, evolution is a perpetual process of adaptation achieved through discarding parts that are useless with regard to the environment and honing only those parts that are effective. However, in the case of URBOT, the meaning of his social existence has been sustained by his uselessness, so his adaptations to the environment are nothing other than the intensification of his useless parts. Perhaps this could be compared to the principle of exaptation in evolutionary theory. Exaptation is the consequence of an excessively direct adaptation to the environment, manifest in phenomena that exceed the level of function and emphasise their symbolic meanings, like the antlers of a deer.

The sense of tension in the evolution of useless spaces arises from an extreme imbalance with the environment due to an increasing friction with reality, and when this tension reaches its peak, URBOT will probably try to reduce it by readapting to the environment through mutation. However, the scale of this avalanche-like phenomenon of mutation is the same as that of the tension arising with regard to the environment, further increasing the vehemence of this vortex of structural transformation. Consequently, the tension generated within URBOT himself is now swelling. I have recurring dreams of a sudden avalanche…

URBOT-001
ALUMINIUM HOUSE

In May 1971, URBOT-001 took root in the concrete rubble on the outskirts of Tokyo.

The fate of URBOT is to be constantly gazing at reality, to be sitting face-to-face with reality, but when he and other people awaken from their dream world they will experience unbearable feelings of being attacked. The accumulated tension toward reality in the process from design through to construction will cause the inhabitants

27

to confront new situations as they experience these spaces with their own bodies. That is to say, the collisions between the spaces of URBOT and the people inhabiting them will add a new level of tension. At first, people will inquisitively enter the spaces of this malformed child with recessive heredity and look askance at the experience of living in unconventional spaces – at the disparity between the exterior walls of reflective aluminium and the somewhat gloomy plywood-lined interiors, the ground floor and the first floor connected through triangular voids containing a cruciform beam surrounded by angle braces, two cylindrical lights further above, a striped carpet in the primary colours red and blue. People encountering this incoherent space will begin to feel confused, indescribably uncomfortable, assailed by annoying sensations, then will finally decide to confront it, in an attempt to make this useless space effective, to transform it into an efficacious and functional space. The resulting deep traces are added to this useless space. But the depth of these traces is undoubtedly the motor for the next stage in the evolution of URBOT.

As I have already mentioned, the spaces of URBOT constantly nurture contradictory conditions in order to exist in the desert-like urban reality. For example, the materiality of the aluminium exterior walls is based upon the contradiction of using a material strongly associated with industrial manufacturing as an element in the production of vernacular architectural spaces. I had wanted to somehow incorporate here the beautiful timber siding that arose in the stream of California vernacularism, but wondered how to integrate it with the steel frames and concrete rubble of the expansive desert of Tokyo. An eccentric feeling of continuity was achieved by cladding the exterior walls with aluminium, or coloured steel sheet.

Even in the space below the two cylinders of light, where the energy conduits have been gathered, the design was begun with the intention of giving expression to information and energy terminals. However, during the design process, URBOT remembered those phrases that might also be called the last words of his parents. If just a single step is taken toward the realisation of a cool world, in which machines are treated as toys, then its radiance will be instantaneously lost. The information terminals were jettisoned right at this moment of hesitation, leaving two useless spaces, like deer antlers. Spaces that are mere empty husks, futilely suffused with light.

URBOT-002
USELESS CAPSULE HOUSE

This is a private home. Enclosed by 10m-long, windowless concrete walls, a single door leads to the interior and a cylindrical shaft of light shines in from a large skylight, directly below which is placed a circular kitchen unit like the *irori* (hearth) found in the middle of an old Japanese *minka* (vernacular house). Beyond this is a row of bed capsules for the family members, as well as a toilet and a bath unit, which comprise the entirety of the facilities in the house.

Though the toilet and the bath unit are no more than 1m square, their ceilings are exceptionally high, and natural light enters from a height of 7m. This also applies to the bed capsules. These unusual spaces, extremely distorted in the vertical direction, have resulted from the evolution of the useless spaces in URBOT-001.

If the family has another child, a bedroom will be given to the newborn baby, though this space should be called a bed capsule rather than a bedroom since it is only large enough to hold one bed. Positioned precisely above the pillow is a tube extending to a height of about 5m, acting as a window. The tube penetrates the roof of the dwelling, and light enters through a skylight inserted in its tip. Depending on the family's financial situation at the time they are made, one bed unit may be marble, another bronze, another pressed steel to which a metallic gold coating has been applied. Opening the car bonnet-like door will alter the location of a small white ball suspended above the pillow on the bed inside. A registration number is etched into the long tube of each capsule, and so even without nameplates a person's location may be ascertained from outside. Furthermore, a capsule will be used throughout its owner's lifetime, and re-registration is necessary in cases of loss or theft. Upon the owner's death, oil is poured into the capsule, the dome of the skylight is detached, and the capsule becomes an incinerator for their cremation. It will then be buried with only the tube projecting above the ground. In other words, the national registration number becomes a *homyo* (posthumous Buddhist name) and the tube is transformed into a grave-marker. The bed capsules are produced in accordance with this ecosystem. Modern dwellings are unable to move because they become filled with too many objects. Nevertheless, like a spaceship, many types of energy and information terminals are brought inside the minimal spaces of these hypothetical capsules. In a private room that ought to be the last refuge for escaping from all systems of control, it was unbearable for URBOT to be controlled under the pretext of being a mechanical capsule. As a consequence, URBOT expelled everything from its own spaces and attempted to resume a relationship with the spaces of the remaining ruins. People slip into the bed capsules of 002 and sleep while illuminated by the faint moonlight transmitted through the tubes from a great height, then greet the sunlight that enters from the same great height. Though everything seems completely normal, they crawl out of their capsules with a kind of ominous premonition. A very unhappy morning has arrived…

URBOT-003
TOKYO VERNACULARISM

One day, a bed capsule from URBOT-002 stepped over the wall of the dwelling and became an independent unit. This was the genesis of the home-sized capsule URBOT-003. Entirely in conformity with the theory of useless evolution,

003 has a citizen registration number inscribed on a light tube that extends far longer than that of 002. Aside from the toilet and shower unit embedded within the walls, the 3.6m-square home-sized capsule contains only a ring-shaped kitchen unit directly below the skylight.

The capsule has only one small entrance and no windows, with pale light shining down through the tube from a hight of 11m. Aside from married couples, this capsule is intended for use by individuals, and one capsule is given to each child when they enter elementary school.

Independent URBOT-003 units are buried in the desert-like vacant lots of Tokyo. As if bubonic plague had struck the city, the scene is of a spreading contagion weaving through the crevices between skyscrapers, covering the roads, covering the plazas, covering the rooftops, covering the surfaces of the expressways. I want you to imagine the appearance of innumerable home-sized capsules with metallic gold cladding emitting a lingering, dull light at sunset in smog-covered Tokyo. Hypothetically, let's position one capsule on each point of a 10m-square grid. If 10 million of these gleaming gold capsules were so positioned, they would fill a square plot of land more than 30km on each side.

In the surroundings of this URBOT-003 array, there are no solid community spaces similar to existing plazas. Rather, the existing plazas and parks have been eroded. Many architects take the word community as the basic unit of urban composition. For local residents this evokes a sweet, beautiful plaza in which they may gather to chat surrounded by water fountains, but for URBOT a modern community is the lowest common denominator arising from selfish human desires: bloody, filthy, hidden in darkness, nothing more than a space as a balancing point fraught with a certain tension. This is absolutely not a beautiful, sweet or calm space, and it is even less likely to be a safe, harmless space. From the outset there was no intention to provide such community spaces. Instead, the spaces around the 003 units will be swallowed and erased within a place and time composed from the equilibrium of shared illusions. They will connect the gaps between the capsules like ripples in the sand – appearing then vanishing, then appearing and vanishing again.

Like the dark clouds of Lem's *The Invincible*, the world of URBOT is precisely this image of an unbroken continuity of gleaming gold 003 units engulfing all the skyscrapers in the desert that is Tokyo.

WHITE RING
(1976)

REALITY

Perhaps what I am now pursuing is the restoration of the architectural act to its most primordial locus: an incision that freely and richly encloses a given field. If the starting point is one's own reality, the resulting architecture will inevitably articulate the reality of its creator in some form, no matter how many constraints are placed upon it.

Previously, I had been attempting to materialise spaces guided by formal manipulations such as axial lines and symmetries, but I felt that I could not accept the division of a large curved wall into left and right by passing a vertical axis through the middle of a U-shaped plan. Even if it resulted in a form with a strong symmetry, the beauty of the gently curving wall surface would be stifled. Following a confrontation between my impulse to define a form with an axis and my extremely sensuous impulse to pursue spatial beauty, I chose the latter.

From the moment that I eliminated the axis and brought the entrance to one end, the interior of this architecture abandoned its linear, rigid spaces and slowly embraced my image of a U-shaped white ring, which guided the development from then on.

Though a trivial discovery in the design process, this was quite an important event because, beyond merely changing the quality of the space, it also affected the design method. Moreover, I felt certain that the result was not motivated by a conceptual operation but was generated from an impetus that was intrinsic to the design.

FLOW AND LAG

When a linear field – 3.6m in width, 2.2-to-3.9m in ceiling height, and about 45m in length – is sealed into a white ring, another field becomes contained on its inner face. These two fields are opposed and completely different in character. The former is a fluid space in which people circulate together with the flows of light and air, and the latter is a space in which everything stagnates. Let's provisionally call them Flow and Lag.

Flow (F) is a closed ring, but rather than a rigid tube it must be a soft and flexible ring. The expression of the flows of air and light, and of the people contained therein, will change over time, and these changing aspects comprise a field in which flows and vortices may be sensed. I wanted to materialise such a field.

In ordinary architecture, spaces intended to enable functions are placed in appropriate locations and then linked by the implementation of connective spaces such as corridors. However, with the exception of a small number of private rooms, that kind of spatial partitioning is absent here. A variety of purposive spaces and connective spaces are gently dissolved within a single field of flow. As a consequence, people carry out their everyday activities within this Flow (F) – that is to say, they inhabit it.

Some architects have raised the question of whether this space somehow already deviates from architecture proper, through its blending of ordinary spatial units into a fluid field. If a conventional architectural configuration is defined as a place for daily life, then certainly this space might be considered to be a deviation from architecture. For me, however, the making of architecture is still the act of seeking the meaning of inhabitation, and so, at one step removed from everyday activity, I want to enquire into what people desire and what causes them grief, and make architecture as a field that may touch on such emotions. Accordingly, I want first to establish a continuous, fluid field, and then make it inhabitable by establishing places for everyday acts.

The white, inorganic space of Flow (F) contrasts with Lag (L), a field of black soil enclosed by a concrete wall. Separated from the external world by two layers of enclosure, air and light both stagnate here, and silence reigns. Any sounds just rebound linearly back and forth between the hard, closed walls. This is a field in which everything may be instantaneously comprehended. When looking up from here toward the skyscrapers of Shinjuku, a person will feel cast into an underground space. Yet even here, the weeds sprout up and the pigeons flutter down.

Flow (F) and Lag (L) are fully contiguous yet nonetheless distantly separated, aside from the relationships through a few tiny apertures. Consequently, this architecture probably cannot be comprehended using the concept of a courtyard house. Nor am I moved in the slightest if someone points out that it resembles a baroque architectural pattern. For me, the only issue is that of two spaces with differing meanings, and the relationship between them. I think that the separation clarifies the character of each field, and also increases the tension in their relationship.

MORPHEME

Flow (F) is materialised as a composition of elements with disparate forms. To gently close the ring, which has a mostly uniform cross-section, one has to implement a sequence of places that allows one to sense the changing rhythm of the diverse elements, however they are distributed and arranged in the ring. Assembled within this field are elements such as arcs with differing radii, neatly stepping walls, three different types of skylight, multiple alcoves, a line of fluorescent lamps that traverses the space, and a circular marble table. A stepping wall is merely a form intended to produce a rhythm. The line of fluorescent lamps and the incised slits of the skylights, detached from the purpose of ensuring brightness, are also just forms, lines of light that traverse this zone. And the large marble table, rather than being functional, may be perceived as having a formal meaning, just one among the many superimposed arcs that give dynamism to the space.

When all of these elements are freed from their respective functional meanings and collected as mere forms, they may be called morphemes. I wanted to adopt the concept of morpheme as a tool for articulating a field detached from functional and rational meanings, no more than suspended units of form unaccompanied by any kind of emotion. If the operation of arranging morphemes may inscribe rhythm and dynamism into a space, then the conventional planning methods of spatial division or connection may be transposed into this entirely different operation of arranging morphemes. Like notating a graphic score in contemporary music, perhaps this operation is the act of distributing neutral symbols. I have only now begun to pursue this new concept, and I cannot yet give it a systematic description. There is the challenge of discovering new morphemes themselves, followed by the task of arranging them and indentifying their integrated structures. The process of identifying these structures is perhaps related to the old theme of urban semiotics.

The New York school of architects, exemplified by figures such as Richard Meier, have attempted to decompose Le Corbusier's architecture into pure forms from which they then extract various elements and recompose them to make their own architecture, but their elements might also be called morphemes. The originality of their compositional methods using these elements allows them to make meaningful contemporary architecture, but personally I prefer to think of morphemes as forms abstracted from the urban and natural scenes contained in my own memory and consciousness. Particularly in these terms, the theme of urban semiotics perhaps gives the impression of an abrupt disjunction of scale in attempting to inscribe the incommensurable city in the small architectural field of a house. However, I am not trying to make architecture as a model of the city, of course, nor would I ever attempt an analogical replication of the form of a part of the city. But the entirety of my daily life takes place in the city, all of its many tangible phenomena accumulate within me as a relationship with the city, and it could even be said that they permeate my bodily rhythms and sense of motion. For me, to express this kind of embodied sensation in architecture is to meaningfully symbolise the city. Architects frequently search for connections between nature and architecture, and attempt to superimpose their own architecture on the historical architecture of Japan and the West. But even if nature and history are today the subjects of wisdom and sentiment, they do not shape the rhythm of my body. This is still shaped by nothing other than the reality of the discrete relationships between the city and myself.

CURVED SURFACES

Despite having said that Flow (F) is a linear zone, the character of this field is undoubtedly dominated by curved wall surfaces.

To begin with, a curved surface induces movement. By delineating a loose curve rather than linear extensions or perpendicular corners, the field of vision constantly changes, the spaces ahead are not presented all at once, and the totality appears only gradually. A person first senses the flows of light, air and sound, and makes a conjecture based on hints about the field extending ahead, then by relying on these hints, steps forward into the conjectured space.

When people circulate through this field, it changes in expression as they glide through a succession of overlapping places without clear boundaries, giving the impression of drifting aimlessly in this time and this field.

In addition to the two curved surfaces ($R_1=7.65m$, $R_2=4.05m$) that define the field, I think the impression of drifting aimlessly in Flow (F) is produced by the interplay of several sizes of arc, implemented as morphemes. While the $R_3=1.98m$ quarter-circle wall encircling the two private rooms is continued by the R4=4.05m arc, there is also a curved wall surface engulfed by the inner face, a small curve that continuously joins the wall to the ceiling, as well as the R5=0.85m table. In this way, one large arc draws out a sequence of other arcs with various radii, which begin to mutually interfere and form a vortex in Flow (F).

The use of curved surfaces appears in many recent houses, but I think there are few instances in which several types of curved surface interfere within the interior in this way, or use the outer face of a curved surface as an interior, like the R2 wall that separates Flow (F) and Lag (L).

Ultimately, it is the largest curved surface, R1, that has the strongest influence on Flow (F). When people walk in this field, it is this wall without apertures that unceasingly meets their eyes. Due to its visual effect, the field appears larger than its actual cross-section. This curved surface is also a screen for reflecting light. It is a curved surface that can even distort light and shadow. In the floor plan, this arc was just drawn mechanically with a compass, but when erected as a curved surface, it affects people not as geometry but as a spatial effect. The curved surface is a morpheme that causes a variety of completely unanticipated outcomes.

LIGHT AND SHADOW

Flow (F) contains three skylights and four clerestories facing onto Lag (L). The differences in position, shape and size of these apertures modulate the quantity, strength, softness and hue of the light drawn into this closed ring, and they are very important elements for giving rhythm to the field.

For example, one skylight is a 45cm-wide slit that crosses the middle of the large curved surface. I have used a similar kind of slit previously (Cottage in Sengataki). However, by cutting between the two curved walls here, tracks of light are projected onto the wall and floor throughout the day, and they unexpectedly change shape.

Early on a sunny morning, a sliver of light – thin, like a Japanese sword with a very slight warp – gradually becomes a broader and stronger linear band that folds from wall to floor, then its width becomes compressed again, and the projected band of the setting sun is extinguished. Once it is gone, only the atmospheric colour of the external world is softly transmitted.

The other six skylights and clerestories are not as precise as that, but each responds to the sun's position and strength, reflecting it in light, shade and hue on the walls and floor. I wanted to notate the distribution of light and shade – incessantly changing according to season and moment – on multiple flat surfaces, in order to make a field of abstract light with a transparency of notation that resembles the distribution of symbols on white paper. Though the apertures engender a gloomy field within this building, it is far from my intention for people here to feel what is referred to as the hidden darkness of ancient Japanese spaces. Nor is this a twilight that conveys the wavering of a candle. Instead of candles, my present intentions are quite precisely expressed by the dry light of slimline fluorescent lamps.

On architectural construction sites, there are many pleasurable discoveries to be made. The sizes of several of the arcs were determined during the building process, and the decision to project the shadows of people on the curved walls came only after construction had made considerable progress. Visiting the site one night, I was inspired by the shadows of the scaffolding planks that had been assembled to apply the wall and ceiling finishes – the many floodlights placed on the rough floor caused bow shapes to be cast on the curved walls.

The three spotlights installed in the floor allow a person walking here at night to play with their three overlapping shadows, which differ in size and colour. Yet for me, this device is more meaningful than playful. Rather than transmitting the gloomy history of family life, what I want from a white wall is no more than a notation of the shapes of people casually leaping about.

The images of light and shadow make it unnecessary to hang paintings in this space. As a person who attempts to grasp architecture in terms of form alone, this seems more natural to me.

WHITE

I finished Flow (F) entirely in white for no other reason than a desire to establish a field like a sheet of white paper on which the distribution of various signs is notated. I was pursuing a white that conveys nothing, a white that could manifest the emptiness of white.

However, meaning inheres in white, and it is not a colour that is easily sullied. It quickly takes on a radiance that is apt to be accompanied by sentimentality and endowed with sweetness. The white of the Villa Savoye, the white of the Schröder House, the white of a cluster of buildings in Mykonos bathed in strong sunlight and facing the azure sea – this whiteness becomes superimposed on the whiteness of easily melted snow. In literature, in painting and in architecture, white is not used as a colour filled with expectations. For me, white possesses a sense of dread that is far from sweet. That is because white summons white. Just as a curved surface conjures another curved surface, I think that magic powers are concealed in white.

In truth, I did not initially intend to cover Flow (F) with so much white. However, once the white began to appear, it dominated everything else. To the extent that the whiteness increased, the remaining parts displayed a heterogeneous presence in a field of pure forms, and conversely appeared to take on strong meanings. The operation of bleaching was undertaken with a feeling of dread that my own reality was being fundamentally tested.

Malevich's depiction of a white square on a white background in 1918 was truly a symbolic event. Here too, his previously depicted forms of black or red squares disappeared into the white. Merely the shadow of their presence was retained in the white field. Beyond being the conclusion of a train of thought, this extreme expression undoubtedly testified to the reality of the presence of the artist. Though I covered all of Flow (F) in white, I decided against covering the exterior of this building with white. The white used on the exterior was limited to small parts such as the entrance door, in order to hint at the white interior. In this architecture, the interior is confined by the operation of making a closed form, so as a consequence it was unnecessary to conceal the exterior with white. It is the deluge of white that necessitates an enquiry into the meaning of white.

SIGNS OF LIGHT
(1977)

This essay is not a paean to light in architecture. Nonetheless, the word light does have an excessively symbolic resonance. The contrast of light and dark has been a dominant theme in the literature, thought and art of Western Europe since medieval times, symbolising brightness and shadow, heaven and earth, life and death, and so on. Even today, the paintings of Rembrandt or Rouault still have the power to trigger a kind of emotional response, drawing us into a mental world.

Yet when making architecture now, however much it may glow with a psychological, inner beauty, the symbolism of light in opposition to darkness cannot be expressed in a space. That is because there are no longer situations in which true darkness is produced. Having said that, a contrast between light and shade is not the intention either. I think this is because we no longer have light strong enough to give an impression of contrast in our surroundings – neither a flickering light floating within dark shadows, nor a strong light dramatising the relief of a rhythmical surface. Instead, we are left with a 'bright world without shadow, or colour, or light sources or even time'.[1] There is no closed cosmos here. Such a world seems truly absurd. All the same, it closely resembles the world in which I live.

No matter how a space is contained in architecture today, even if it is intended to depict an individual's inner world, one could say that it is impossible to compose a self-contained cosmos. Rather, even if containment is attempted, the effect of a condition of porosity or leakage will probably turn the act of making into nothing more than various methods of signification.

Living in a city like Tokyo, just walking through underground passageways or along the base of tall buildings, one has almost no awareness of exterior light. When inside an office building, one is aware of sunlight coming in the windows and of the blue of the sky, but even those things do not linger in the mind at the day's end.

But if one goes somewhat higher than ground-level sightlines, such as the rooftop of a six- or seven-storey building, one invariably looks out at the silhouette of a cluster of skyscrapers. Viewed from the rear rooftop of the apartment building in which I live, only a few kilometres away from Shinjuku, the setting sun hits the clusters of skyscrapers, each returning a dully reflected light, like a single sheet of metal or glass, and the building shadows stretch over the surrounding area for many hundreds of metres, sometimes extending to more than a kilometre.

The cars running along the roads below also sometimes emit a dull light, and the sheet-steel roofs of the wooden houses that engulf the lower parts of the buildings can be seen gleaming here and there. Projecting only their upper parts from between the wooden houses, the glass surfaces of the small-to-medium-sized buildings, and the billboards attached to their rooftops, emit a slightly stronger reflected light. Even the trees that may be glimpsed between the buildings seem achromatic rather than green, merely glittering and sparkling. Though definitely not strong, most of this reflected light forms a vast fabric of soft light comprising an array of shining points.

Though every part of this city has been coated with gaudy colours, all of these colours are absorbed by the sunlight and become an almost monochrome fabric. The infinite distribution of light conveys a certain lambency, but rather than a vivid radiance like innumerable points of light reflected on water, it's a wavering of almost colourless points, like Claude Monet's late work *Water Lilies*. To be sure, these scenes also contain intensities and colours that differ according to the season. But throughout the changing seasons, even on very sunny days, the sun is dull and rarely gives an impression of clarity. In the soft background, as if wrapped in gauze, there is always a sense of anomie. Also clearly distinct from the fleeting impressions found in the delicately depicted rural scenes in Japanese-style paintings, this sensation is perhaps the characteristic expression of light in this city.

I look out over the overcrowded residential districts that extend everywhere, in which the inhabitants brandish the slogan 'don't steal our sun' and undoubtedly even today continue their disputes over rights to sunshine. Despite the opaque sunlight of Tokyo, in the daily life of its people the sun is turned into a symbol and worshipped. Or perhaps, it is rather precisely because of the weakness of the rays of light that the sun is made spiritual and symbolic.

When making architecture in this city, even in the smallest of houses, I will sever a piece of the fabric of light being produced by the city, and there enclose a field. For me, the only possible action is then to turn the severed, interwoven cross-sections into signs within this field. These signs are absolutely not converted into symbols. The aspects of light shifting together with the passage of time are codified into various tangible expressions. These are not incorporated within the system of meanings that exist in daily life, but are intended to become a fresh collection of codes of light. People absorb this collection of codes as they walk, and perhaps when the absorbed codes are rewoven inside each person, the field will begin to gain meaning through the medium of light.

Soon after I had begun the design of the House in Nakano Hommachi, the topic of the light in the spaces arose during a discussion with the client – who I should say was my older sister, then engaged in work on the history of music. She showed me a small book by Hidemichi Tanaka, titled *Fuyu no Yami* [*The Darkness of Winter*], and talked about the paintings of the early seventeenth-century French artist Georges de La Tour, a contemporary of the Dutch artists Rembrandt and Van Dyck. That was when I first heard the name of the artist La Tour, who spent his life in the Lorraine region during the early Baroque era.

Throughout his life, La Tour is said to have depicted not a single landscape, but only human beings. Moreover, these human beings were all set against a background of jet-black darkness, and brought into view by the flickering light of a candle. The most impressive work by this artist is a series of paintings depicting the conversion of the penitent Mary Magdalene. Titled *Magdalen of the Night-Light*, *Magdalen with the Smoking Flame*, and so on, all of them depict Mary Magdalene sitting on a chair in front of a candle with a wavering white flame, which is placed upon a desk. In *Magdalen with the Smoking Flame*, the burning candle flame is reflected in a mirror placed upon the same desk. Only her long, black hair, the white clothes on her torso, and her skin are illuminated within the darkness, surrounding which is a static space. However, a skull is placed upon the young woman's knee. The whiteness of her skin – as if made from alabaster – suggests a female figure contemplating death, pulling our gaze into the tranquil darkness, and we are quickly captivated by this extraordinary world.

La Tour's world of darkness, in an era still without artificial light, was itself the world of night. For the solitary spirit unable to sleep on long, dark nights, the burning light had a character of consolation and was at the same time a symbol of uneasiness … fire is life, but if extinguished then darkness returns, and all that remains is the fear of death. Only the skull that La Tour depicted on the knee of the saint is not a symbol of death. The candle flame itself anticipates death.[2]

Though I had been deeply moved by the flickering white flames depicted by La Tour, the only light that illuminates the spacious hall in my sister's house comes from one long, slender fluorescent lamp and three spotlights. The former is a line of white light that runs in midair through the room, and the latter were installed as graphical projection light-sources that cast the silhouettes of human beings onto a white wall. Both types of light are far removed from the white flames of a candle. Within a white space, they do not emerge from within the darkness, and they are not conveyed by trembling shadows. Unlike the subdued shadows projected onto old *shoji* screens, the silhouettes are crisp mixtures of blue and yellow projected on hard, white walls, and traces never linger. Some people may think that these lights are inorganic, abstract, inhumanly cold, lacking in vitality. However, I can only say that to adopt such an expressive method is to come as close as possible to the meaning of making architecture today. For me, it is now no longer possible to bring into architecture the medieval light found in La Tour's work.

By way of comparison with La Tour, who only depicted the light of night, the artist who immediately comes to mind as having most beautifully depicted the light of day is probably the Dutchman Johannes Vermeer, who was born in 1632, only about 40 years after La Tour, and ended his short, 40-year lifespan in Delft. The experiences of these two painters may be felt in the serenity and transparency of the light they depicted.

Vermeer also painted many young women. However, these women are always depicted within everyday life – intently reading a letter, or wearing an apron and pouring milk from a jar, or weaving lace, or weighing pearls with a scale. Compared to La Tour's depiction of Mary Magdalene, shrouded in moribund silence, the expressions of the women appearing in Vermeer's work are bright and enveloped with a sense of wellbeing. Common to most of the pictures is a window at the left side of the frame, throwing subdued light on these women in gloomy rooms. The softness and beauty of the transparent light fixes the movement of the various gestures made by the women, giving them a radiance and immortality.

In Vermeer's case, it is the windows that make light into a symbol. In his townscapes *View of Delft* and *The Little Street*, these windows, viewed from the building exteriors, are no more than simple leaded glass framed by thick pieces of wood. Yet looking out from inside the room, they begin to momentarily shine, permeated by infinitely changing light. In many cases, the glass is subdivided by a delicate lattice of straight lines and curves, occasionally set with glass coloured like medieval rose windows. The weak light of northern Europe is softened even further when it penetrates these delicate windows; sometimes the whiteness of the fabric wrapping the girl's head seems to float, and sometimes the blue and yellow clothing makes a vivid impression. The area around the inside of the window is mostly tinged a pale bluish-purple and pale yellow close to white, delineating a field of light suffused with a sense of transparency. I cannot help thinking that the interior field of beautiful light recalls the peaceful townscape depicted in *View of Delft*, with its rows of red-and-blue coloured roofs. More than a portrayal of a specific place, might it be said that the scenes depicted by Vermeer comprise an eternal imaginary landscape that lies within each of us?

However, as long as this imaginary landscape is repressed within us, it should be kept in mind that the act of building even now begins by excising a spot from this landscape.

Incidentally, as beautiful as the light expressed by Vermeer may be, I find it an interesting conjecture that he may have used a camera obscura when painting these pictures. This was an era of rapid development in a wide range of scientific thought – through figures such as Descartes, Kepler, Galileo, even Huygens – and given the remarkable advances in lens-making in this region, it is no wonder that some artists used this optical equipment in an attempt to give their observations a greater objectivity. As Mitsuhiko Kuroe writes:

In Vermeer's time, the camera obscura was already in use, implemented as one thin reflector placed between the lens and the ground glass from above, bending the light rays ... The light passing through the inside of the camera obscura hits a translucent screen. The screen projects the vivid colours of nature, like a bright window. It is a small window of light.

The light of the window reflects the window of light. While twisting the lens, Vermeer stared at the flickering light of the window within the light... The familiar windows, maps, carpets, paving, yellow clothing with fur attached, woven fabric curtains, chairs decorated with lions, musical instruments and so on, while often appearing in the field of view, always emit differing glows. While the artist used familiar objects, as well as his wife Catharina and their children, as models, when contained within the 'window of light' they were recombined into an image of a world in which time is paused.[3]

Even if this is no more than guesswork, it is deeply interesting to think that the interior world of an artist may have come into being through the intermediary of optical equipment. The fact that Vermeer did not depict the world of religion, but only everyday scenes, certainly suggests the presence of a camera obscura. The translucent screen of a 'window of light' would perhaps vividly, yet truthfully, signify the world of three-dimensional light on a two-dimensional surface. The accurate images projected on this screen were idealised on canvas as eternal light, and undoubtedly Vermeer still had an intrinsic sense of medieval light. Through this act of symbolisation, Vermeer's work attains a universal value.

However, the medieval light that glowed so feverishly within Vermeer is now nowhere to be found. All that remains for us is light as a code projected onto a translucent screen.

In terms of the desire to expose architecture to the bright, perpetual light of the modern era, beyond concept and beyond expression, Le Corbusier is probably the superlative example. Truly, when confronted with Le Corbusier's paeans to the sun throughout the 1920s and 1930s, replete with convictions and expectations, it is impossible to avoid feeling a kind of guilt, as if witnessing one's own panic at being dragged from darkness into the light of day.

The first draft of *Towards a New Architecture* was written in 1920–21, but as many people have already pointed out, all of the architecture mentioned – in Greece, Ancient Rome, Egypt, Pompeii – existed under Mediterranean light. Certainly his many pure white dwellings of the 1920s, including the Villa Savoye, were composed as collections of elements with primary geometric shapes such as cubes and cones, and these shapes appear most radiant when exposed to strong beams of light. It seems that his interest in light during that period was directed at the primary shapes of the exterior rather than the interior spaces, as these extracts from *Towards a New Architecture* show.

Architecture being the masterly, correct and magnificent play of masses brought together in light, the task of the architect is to vitalize the surfaces that clothe these masses... Our eyes are made to see forms in light... The elements of architecture are light and shade, wall and space... Rome is a picturesque spot. The sunlight there is so beautiful that it excuses everything... The light plays on pure forms and repays them with interest. Simple masses develop immense surfaces which display themselves with a characteristic variety according as it is a question of cupolas, vaulting, cylinders, rectangular prisms or pyramids... The Egyptian pyramids, of granite once polished and shining like steel, were moving... The walls are in full brilliant light, or in half shade or in full shade, giving an effect of gaiety, serenity or sadness. Your symphony is made ready.[4]

These words are utterly bereft of shadows. And this brightness is then replaced by the expectation of a new way of life based on functionality and rationality. 'Demand a bathroom looking south, one of the largest rooms in the house or flat, the old drawing-room for instance. One wall to be entirely glazed, opening if possible on to a balcony for sun baths.' 'Teach your children that a house is only habitable when it is full of light and air, and when the floors and walls are clear.'[5]

Regardless whether or not the strong Mediterranean light beloved by Le Corbusier actually exists here in Japan, this Corbusian light, rather than illuminating primary shapes in contemporary architecture, is more commonly shone on the functional aspects of everyday life. It appears terribly indifferent as a result, particularly in interior spaces, with the only concern being to make every nook and cranny bright and comfortable, as opposed to producing beautifully lit interiors. This tendency continues even today, and there are few examples of architecture in which the treatment of interior light is worth looking at.

Incidentally, during the 1930s Le Corbusier's treatment of light in his architecture begins to show a gradual change. Where previously he created flat surfaces comprising solid walls and glazing in the same plane, he now uses methods that emphasise the strong contrast of light and shade by making deep mouldings in the vertical surfaces, aiming for the effect of light as a mass. The surface finishes shift from white plaster to rough, bare concrete. Thick, upward-curving concrete eaves, exemplified by the architecture of Chandigarh, became a popular design motif here in Japan for a brief period, but even so, I think that without the strong sunlight of India it was less successful.

Rather than these methods of changing the exterior wall treatments in relation to the external light, what interests me more is the darkness engendered within the architecture of Le Corbusier from the 1950s on, and the light that shines into these spaces of darkness. For example, at Notre Dame du Haut (that is to say, Ronchamp Chapel), the gently curving wall surfaces, in their extraordinary thickness, already seem to me to exceed the concept of wall. They are pierced by various large holes, from which multiple lines of light extend in accordance with the size of the aperture, merging softly in the interior, accompanied by the colours of the stained glass fixed into the window… And while the exterior forms of the towers above the altar are obviously associated with the Mediterranean, when one is inside, looking up, one gets the sense of being in a deep cavern or the womb of a giant animal.

Or take the monastery of La Tourette. To imagine the darkness that dominates this architecture and the spaces of primary-coloured light that emerge within it, I first read the words of Arata Isozaki.

Receiving the rhythmic stimulus of light falling through forest-like vertical mullions called pans *de verre ondulatoires*, spaced according to the Modulor, along the ramp connected to the labyrinthine corridors which weave through the monks' quarters surrounding the inner courtyard, abruptly entering an underground corridor where you can only move by groping in the darkness, then encountering the scene of a glowing altar painted in primary colours illuminated by the *canons de lumière* – in other words, a bundle of light tubes – for me, more than surprise, I was intoxicated by a kind of ecstasy that I want to record here.

It was absolutely a scene from the ocean depths. Exterior light is brought in through holes cut at various angles, and several of the tubes have been painted in colours on the inner faces, on which light reflects and becomes tinged with primary colours. I imagined that human beings were being forced to swim among various objects that faintly appeared within the space demarcated by untreated, rough *béton brut* surfaces. And when confronting the red, yellow and black painted walls, my impression was that the monks were surely having sexual intercourse with God.[6]

Isozaki explains that this space replete with Eros, to the extent that it can be considered sexual, is an expression of Le Corbusier's physical body itself, which loved the sea and departed in its embrace. In driving the physical body to its absolute limits against this background, Eros appears, and when this occurrence includes a space of worship, I cannot help but think that the light in this architectural interior is still oriented toward the medieval. As much as this architect extolled bright, strongly transparent light, in his final years he secretly pursued a profoundly dark space. Why was so much of the light finally medieval? In the middle of the 1930s, in *When the Cathedrals were White*, he beautifully expressed the 'white, limpid, joyous, clean, clear' qualities of medieval light, but perhaps the shadows were already visible at this time, coinciding with a medieval period in which people were being dragged into the abyss.

When I built my first work, Aluminium House, just five years ago, the way light is brought inside the architecture was already an important theme for me. The two cylinders that characterise the exterior form of this house were installed only for illumination, and aluminium was used to clad the entire exterior on the assumption that it would be struck by the subdued sunlight of this city and reflect it back as a dull light. Though the light drawn in through these two cylinders may not seem particularly effective in the interior space, it provided many hints for the manipulation of light in subsequent designs.

As I have already mentioned, for me the theme of light is a question of how to signify in architecture the expression of light in this city. In concrete terms, it became two curved surfaces: one is related to the method of codifying light on wall and floor surfaces, and the other is the relation of light to the composition of those surfaces.

When thinking about the codification of light on surfaces, I cannot avoid the problem of superficiality. In two of my house designs, the Cottage in Sengataki and the House in Nakano Hommachi, direct sunlight from a skylight strikes a white wall and projects various shapes. The wall surfaces – in the former case, freestanding in the centre of the room and reaching the ceiling, in the latter case, formed by two gradually curved surfaces – are made from entirely rigid materials, and rather than wall surfaces they are better described simply as abstract, plain screens. I think that conventional wall surfaces have always been conceived in relation to the shadows caused by surface relief modelling being exposed to light. Even in cases without strong contrasts, such as Le Corbusier's facades in which the glass surfaces are set deep in the apertures, there is the problem of the expression of the delicate nuances of light hitting the roughness of the materials. Certainly, strange shadows arise when bricks or rough plastered surfaces receive light, and these gain a vitality that might be called sensual in gloomy interior spaces.

This sensation of vitality always causes deep contemplation, and the aspiration to somehow touch history. Even as history gradually changes shape, it repeatedly appears before our eyes. Moreover, even within the confines of architectural history, if a situation begins to reach an impasse, it will emerge to the extent that it is described as necessary. But rather than have recourse to this kind of history, might we not instead express the era in which we are immersed?

In these houses I attempted to show, on surfaces as plain as sheets of paper, the various expressions of this urban light, that is to say, the strength of the light, its shape and softness, the hues of direct sunlight cut by slits. This is a graphic image produced by light. In exactly the same way, artificial lighting after nightfall projects the silhouettes of people and furniture here. However, these graphic patterns can never constrain the shapes. The images projected change from moment to moment. When the sun hides itself among the clouds, the large, white screen loses brightness, like *sumi* ink blotting into *washi* paper. With each passing moment, there is no more than the projection of changing figures, endlessly sliding across the surfaces. There is absolutely no meaning being conveyed by what seeps from the inner surfaces of the walls.

The superficiality of images passing in succession across the outer surfaces of walls and floors might be evoked by textures such as printed plywood and vinyl leather. The wood grain applied to printed plywood or the gloss of vinyl leather is no more than a codification of natural materials such as timber and fabric. This method, which attempts to repel the senses of smell and touch and to convey meaning only by the sense of sight, is more than mere falsehood: it entirely engulfs our surroundings. What should be called an era of superficiality could also be called a cultural condition.

But what is a surface? Is it not something that eludes all categories of existence? Surface escapes from the context of ontology, in that, almost by definition, surface cannot become the subject of ontology. A surface has no thickness, and without sending or receiving any background (because the background is also a surface) it evades all depth – and then, people will probably contemptuously describe it as superficial.

Atsushi Miyakawa[7]

European contrasts of light and darkness, or light and shadow, are said to have arisen entirely through the medium of stone. Darkness was accumulated by piling up and enclosing massive stones, and those stones were pierced to draw in light. Moreover, the contrast of light and shadow was caused by the thickness of the stacked stones. This is precisely an aesthetic of depth and thickness. Even Le Corbusier, the progenitor of modern architecture, was unable to escape these limits with regard to light. In the minds of those of us who have already seen Western Europe, the thickness of the stone and the depth of the spaces enclosed by that thickness is undoubtedly miraculous. Yet at the same time, we must not forget we are living within a completely opposite condition of superficiality.

If the sign of light on a surface is taken as a question of superficiality, a field composed by these surfaces is a question of light flows, as well as the rhythms produced by light.

For example, in the case of the House in Sakurajosui, the somewhat-dark living room, approximately 25m square in area, is enclosed by a pure white wall set in front of the entrance, and the light-soaked stairway visible within has been placed so as to create contrast. This is a contrast between the brightness and darkness of the spaces. Moreover, in the case of the House in Nakano Hommachi, the interior is composed as a 3.6m-wide, slowly curving, linear toroidal space, so the rhythm of brightness and darkness is clarified. Brightness and darkness alternate across the bright field of the inner face of the small arc that one must follow to enter the child's room; the long, narrow, dark passage; the extremely bright field below the slit in the roof; the somewhat gloomy field enclosing the small engulfing arc toward the interior; the bright dining area that faces the courtyard; then again to the dark, long passage and the corner that it meets, illuminated by the skylight. The rhythm of these spaces is emphasised by elements that may be called morphemes, though the bright fields and the dark fields are not clearly distinguished but merge into one another, and the overall light is a mixture of flow and lag. People say that when they linger in a corner of this relentlessly white field, the enclosing walls and ceiling do not feel like clear boundaries, and they are drawn into this vague body of light. It is neither a space of darkness nor one filled with the light of the modern era. Being inside this field of subdued light is like being inside a white cloud of intersecting brightness and darkness, which is, as I quoted at the outset, 'a bright world without shadow, colour and light source, or even time'.

It would be false to say that I do not possess an inherent yearning for medieval light. It engendered La Tour's and Vermeer's beautiful works, and finally even Le Corbusier secreted such a world of light within his devilish path. But for me now, I reiterate here the futility of this persistent yearning.

NOTES

1. Eiji Usami, *Meiro no oku* [*Depths of the Maze*] (Tokyo: Misuzu Shobo, 1975).
2. Hidemichi Tanaka, *Fuyu no yami* [*The Darkness of Winter*] (Tokyo: Shinchosensho, 1972).
3. Mitsuhiko Kuroe, *Vermeer* (Tokyo: Shinchosha, 1975).
4. Le Corbusier, *Towards a New Architecture* (New York: Dover, 1986 [1931]).
5. Ibid.
6. Arata Isozaki, 'Eros, or the Sea' in *GA II: Le Corbusier, Couvent Sainte-Marie de La Tourette* (Tokyo: ADA Edita, 1971).
7. Atsushi Miyakawa, *In'yo no orimono* [*Woven Quotations*] (Tokyo: Chikuma Shobo, 1975).

SILVER HUT
(1989)

I was out drinking with Hiroshi Hara and Osamu Ishiyama
one evening, and we started talking about the impoverished images of futuristic cities that appear in science-
fiction film sets, and wondered if we could improve on
them. Following on from that occasion, we were joined
by Riken Yamamoto and Shin Takamatsu for a five-person
symposium titled 'Floating Gardens and Spaceships –
Launching the Image of Architecture for the 21st Century'
(*Kenchiku Bunka*, March 1984). In order to make visionary
depictions of futuristic architectural images, we each first
engaged in a critical debate with two outsiders. The results
were later published as 'Architecture – Predictions for
Tomorrow' (*Kenchiku Bunka*, March 1986 special issue).
Though this was intended to become an ongoing series
of publications, laziness on the part of the architects meant
that we never got further than the first edition, yet the
symposium and debates seem to have provided us with
a great deal of impetus.

Hiroshi Hara and Osamu Ishiyama rebuked me for
'leading us toward a world of serenity', and when I heard
them say this I became pensive. Despite being an optimist,
my brooding kept me awake that night, even though I
had been drinking. The validity of architectural criticism
is gauged by the discovery of metaphorical phrases to
describe the works, which are then used as a basis for
celebrating them, or, with regard to those forms that arise
mostly from my own intuitions, for locating them within
contemporary thought. However, beyond such an interpre-
tation of what those two said that evening, our conversa-
tion led to the topic of what they considered to be an ideal
state of architecture.

Hiroshi Hara began to talk about the transparent, sacred spaces in the villages of the minority people of the Lobi tribe, who live on the savanna, and the 'not-not' world of the Upanishads, that is to say, the Buddhist notion of emptiness – an absorbing world without defined order, in contrast to the reflecting world of geometrical order – and so on, which he expanded into a magnificent philosophical field of view. In response, Ishiyama linked the discussion from architecture that takes on the appearance of nature as its guiding principle to the medieval world of Japanese epic poetry, and the two of them arrived at a vision of architecture with a sense of absence, with no progress, no despair, just the condition of stasis itself, as may be felt in this poem by Teika Fujiwara:

Gazing into the distance   *Miwataseba /*
No flowers   *Hana mo momiji mo /*
Nor autumn leaves…   *Nakari keri…*

As Ishiyama pointed out, for me there is an unconscious world as well as a constant desire to instinctively maximise the unconscious. Perhaps this is because I sense a kind of weakness in many pioneering designers who, while aspiring toward the avant-garde of modern architecture, seem ultimately to have reverted to the world of Japanese refinement. After the House in Kasama, I thought about changing my method, and it might be said that I have been instinctively avoiding sophistication. However, from 1980 on, in constantly thinking about the theme of reconceiving architecture in terms of the actions of daily life, I concluded that my aim should be architecture that resembles the existing conditions and reflects human actions in space, so that the question of comfort, as a minimisation of pressure on the human body, will be manifest as a disorderly stack of absorbing spaces. As ever, my architectural arena is still urban space, but I have no desire to replicate the tumultuous spaces of the city, with things in a state of dissonance and tension. I just want to make highly innovative presentations of architecture in its most natural state.

57

WHAT IS THE REALITY OF ARCHITECTURE IN A FUTURISTIC CITY? (1988)

CITY WITHOUT AN EXTERIOR

When visiting a new place, my impression of the city is mostly gained during the process of travelling from the airport to the town centre. That is how stimulating this route can be. The various characteristics and expressions of any city will appear, enveloping and devouring visitors. Sometimes we are met by smiling geniality, and other times we are confronted by a brutal wall blocking our way. Alternatively, we plunge into the city's embrace as if violently sucked up by an enormous vacuum cleaner. Though we cannot predict the kinds of people we will meet and the kinds of events we will encounter, the degree of excitement provided by the city is mostly decided at that moment.

For example, visiting New York for the first time I went directly from JFK airport to my hotel in Manhattan by yellow cab. It was a rainy night. The black driver was humming along to the jazz flowing from the car radio, and then he began to tap the steering wheel with one hand. The windscreen wipers screeched back and forth, curiously keeping pace with the rapid beat of the music. Suddenly, the night view of Manhattan, which I had held in my mind like a picture postcard, appeared beyond the fan pattern that the wipers were delineating.

Or when visiting Bangkok, I was engulfed by a space of extreme humidity with an indescribable fragrance while still at the airport. It was like the air you suddenly breathe when entering a Roman bath, a space filled with the dense fragrances produced when all types of substances are fermenting. Amid the bougainvillea flowers blooming between the private houses, encircled by racing tuk-tuks making strange noises and blowing smoke, my body gradually merged into this flamboyant city. It's an urban space with a softly pulsating rhythmic flow. In the process of yielding to this graceful atmosphere, my sense of smell played a greater role than my sense of sight.

Whether welcoming or rebuffing, whether visual or olfactory, there is a countenance appropriate for each city. London, Barcelona, Mexico City, Shanghai, Sydney, Jakarta – every one of these cities displays this countenance through the totality of its characteristic structures, densities, atmospheres and commercial activities. What is so thrilling about the journey from the airport to the city centre is perhaps this instinctive perception of the overall appearance of the unseen city in which we are being immersed. Only Tokyo is a case apart.

Landing at Narita Airport, one takes a limousine bus and goes by highway to the city centre. There are hotels situated between mountain forests and cultivated fields, vernacular houses and convenience stores, warehouses, small apartment buildings – this mixed, nondescript landscape continues interminably. It cannot be called natural or artificial; if it is unaggressive it has no reason to gently embrace people; if it lacks the sharpness of Manhattan it also lacks the lushness of Bangkok.

It could be called an impoverished landscape, yet while people are examining this utterly desultory landscape – lacking in any deep emotional impact and providing no kind of stimulus – they suddenly find themselves inside the city of Tokyo. In other words, one does not clearly see the countenance of the city, but becomes incorporated in its body before any intuitive impressions are gained.

This lack of stimulation in the approach route cannot be entirely the result of overfamiliarity. First-time visitors to the city will undoubtedly have this same desultory impression of being immersed in a bottomless swamp. A city without an exterior, and a labyrinthine interior that one inadvertently enters at some point: this is the mysterious character of the city called Tokyo.

THE FUTURE DEPICTED BY THE MODERNISTS, AND THE FUTURISM OF THE CONTEMPORARY CITY

Manhattan was once considered the most futuristic of cities. The silhouettes of its urban spaces, resembling clusters of icicles made from steel and glass, are surely manifestations of the skyscrapers drawn by Mies van der Rohe around 1920. These images of architecture rising like a mirage behind a grimy, heavy city made of brick and stone were a lone architect's dream of a future city oriented toward unprecedented spaces. Sustained by a faith in technology, Mies devoted his entire life to gradually assimilating and implementing fictional architectural, or urban, images. Manhattan embodied Mies's dream of urban space as a direct product of the twentieth century, in keeping with his own words: 'Architecture is the will of the epoch translated into space'.

Le Corbusier also depicted unprecedented future spaces set in opposition to the real city. In the video *Le Corbusier*, produced by Jacques Barsac, computer graphics are used to spectacularly present the contrast between reality and the futuristic, illusionistic qualities of the Contemporary City for Three Million Inhabitants (1921–22) and the Plan Voisin for Paris (1925). Exactly like Mies van der Rohe's drawings of skyscrapers, these future cities gleam palely yet brilliantly against the real townscape of Paris.

The future images of cities drawn by modernist architects such as Mies and Le Corbusier, or even those found in Manhattan itself, are all just manifestations of dream cities that deny reality. The future city projects enthusiastically drawn by Japanese architects during the 1960s are no different. However, from the 70s on, architects stopped drawing future cities; astonished by the huge discrepancies between the visions they were drawing and the rapid developments of reality, they all turned away from the city.

Meanwhile, transformation piled upon transformation in our lived urban spaces, which became completely different from those once desired by architects, though they could still be called extremely futuristic. In Tokyo, the skyscrapers in the neighbourhood of West Shinjuku evoke a miniature Manhattan, yet their perceived futuristic quality does not stem from these visual factors but rather from the invisible urban spaces conveyed to our bodies by a diverse set of signals. The architect's task of drawing the future city is no longer based on a desire to draw unprecedented spaces opposed to reality, but is now the visualisation of images captured by means of filters – that is to say, haptic or auditory sensors – within the invisible spaces of reality itself.

This is frankly revealed by the fact that it is filmmakers rather than architects who are today depicting future cities. The medium of film comprises various techniques that are more suitable for depicting invisible urban spaces. It is only natural that architects, being limited to static two-dimensional graphics or three-dimensional models, cannot depict the future.

However, even when movies take extremely futuristic cities as their setting, they actually show real urban spaces, as an examination of the images projected on the screen reveals. In most cases, from *Blade Runner* to *Akira*, they show clusters of huge skyscrapers alternating with the underbelly of the city, which tends toward dilapidated ruins. In depicting these two differing types of spaces, they resemble the drawings of Mies and Le Corbusier, but the groups of skyscrapers that appear on screen are a long way from the beautiful, dream-like architecture depicted with computer graphics in Barsac's *Le Corbusier* video. Instead, they surely approximate real scenes in places such as Shinjuku or Hong Kong. Seeing these skyscrapers in close-up reveals spaces enclosed by columns arrayed like a Mayan temple, or spaces lined with steel pipes like the huge locomotive that appears in the film *Metropolis* – a concealed nostalgia, linked with memories of the past. So why do we feel that scenes showing reality itself, or retreating to portrayals of the recent past, are futuristic?

What suddenly transforms these nostalgic images into futuristic images is the extraordinary increase in the scale of the clusters of skyscrapers, the extraordinary speed of movement from scene to scene in urban space, the accompanying noises and musical rhythms, the spaces woven with innumerable laser beams, all produced by the technological trickery characteristic of cinema. By being cast into these utterly artificial spaces, the real city achieves a magnificent transformation into a future city suffused with fiction. The 'Spinner' flying vehicle in *Blade Runner* and Kaneda's motorcycle in *Akira* – equipped with a Superconducting Generator that allows it to reach a maximum speed of 243km/h, equivalent to a bullet train – are both manifestations of the speeds and rhythms of the future metropolis. There are occasional shots showing aerial views of the city, but such scenes do not play a substantial role in enhancing its futuristic character. Immersed within the city, futuristic urban spaces are achieved just through the experience of topological space, like running around in an endless jungle, or riding a labyrinthine rollercoaster.

FICTIONS PRODUCED BY TECHNOLOGY

In this kind of movie, all the characteristics of a city like present-day Tokyo are contained in the discrepancies between those nostalgic images that can be experienced and the future cities that cannot be depicted by an architect. For example:

1. The relentless transformation into a labyrinth: The feeling of drifting through a complex space mounted on a futuristic vehicle is similar to that of driving a car on the highway. Surrounded by limitless undulating folds, incessantly accelerating, looking up from the valleys toward the building tops, incessantly elongating. There is pleasure in moving freely in both horizontal and vertical directions within this expanding labyrinth. Just as the same

townscape appears completely different when observed while walking or from a car, by adding accelerated vertical movement, it becomes a distant, extraordinary space.

2. Spaces filled with noises produced by technology: The city atmosphere is suffused with a variety of sounds, colours, information and odours. These are not necessarily visualised but are mediated by technology and dispersed in the atmosphere, distributed in urban space with changing densities, like floating clouds or mist. In the movies, due to the appearance of humans with psychic abilities and androids, these atmospheric properties are discerned and recognised, but within the city, we can only adumbrate them with an intensified sense of hearing or touch. Arguably, composers and writers interpret this invisible urban atmosphere with a far keener sensitivity than do architects.

3. An insubstantial world comprising only innumerable suspended symbols of consumption and the sequences of events between them: From ancient times, we Japanese have had the ability to instantly produce spaces corresponding to activities. Japanese methods of spatial conception are clearly demonstrated by examples such as ceremonial spaces created through the simple act of drawing a curtain, or a seating area for a tea ceremony created merely by placing a parasol above a red carpet. The same applies to the empty spaces in traditional wooden houses, where the installation of furniture and other items creates temporary spaces for various activities. These types of spaces, continuously improvised in accordance with events, may be considered essential elements of our urban space. Today, conformity with intrinsic ownership is replaced by a symbolic recognition of the consumption of space, producing the superficial potency and allure of the city. Up to ten years ago, the advertis-

ing signs in commercial spaces were no more than billboards or window displays, or at most affixed to the facades of buildings, but now they occupy entire interior spaces or even cover entire buildings. All urban spaces have now begun a cycle of incessantly changing signs of consumption.

4. Temporal cities created by the trails of bodies: Unreal spaces are produced through successions of events that are like fireworks set off throughout the city, which is sustained by a sense of distance completely different from the perspective and hierarchy of Western space. It might be more appropriate to say that there is no sense of physical distance. This is comparable to the differing spatial cognition of the opera house and the Nō theatre. In the former, the distance, visual orientation and location of the audience seating and the stage all have a tangible meaning – that is to say, it is assumed that audience space will extend radially with the stage as the focus. However, in the latter, the space is treated more abstractly. In each location, the physical distance and orientation of the seats and the stage is abstracted, and each point is just suspended in empty space. That is, wherever one sits, the space is conceived so as to link the viewers in an abstract relationship with the actors. Our urban spaces are similar. In choosing successive performance spaces for our bodies, it is precisely the trails that link our bodies that become urban spaces for each person. Accordingly, the total urban space can be described as the infinitely interwoven spaces of linear trails that are selected and linked by each person.

REALITY AND THE FREEDOM OF ARCHITECTURE

A city without an exterior, a labyrinthine city filled with invisible technologies like fog in the air, a city that begins to make visible the spaces of the inhabitants choosing and linking their successive performances – how should we live comfortably in this kind of fictional, futuristic city, and what kind of architecture should we build there? All the difficulties we confront when living in this city come from the fact that, on the one hand, we are floating in the space of unreal images and, on the other hand, we are, as ever, living in everyday reality. Certainly, viewed from one angle our lifestyle is that of nomads floating in a fictional city. We walk through streets scattered with symbols of consumerism, cycling from restaurant to boutique, to fitness club, to convenience store, to theatre. Strolling from fiction to fiction across dream stage spaces, we may revel in a futuristic urban life.

And it may be said that through this process our bodies are also being transformed to fit these fictional spaces suffused with technology. By touching and inhaling the atmosphere of sounds and rhythms, lights and breezes formed through the medium of technology, there is every reason to think of our consciousness, our senses of touch, hearing and smell, and even our flesh, as becoming android-like. Actually, we have far more affinity with the replicants wearing plastic clothes than with the 'blade runner' detective, and his human stench, in the eponymous film. And so we enviously turn our gaze toward the store mannequins that so resemble replicants. However, that inexpressible discomfort and perplexity we feel when we dress our bodies with the designer clothes worn by those mannequins is the alienation of the dual body located in the gap between the living body and the android body.

To the extent that our bodies are becoming androids, we are forced to adopt a dual sensitivity. In the same way, to the extent that the city is becoming futuristic and fictional, we are forced to adopt a dual lifestyle. It may be fine to selfishly continue inhabiting urban space in a nomadic way, but even as we pursue fleeting, provisional spaces we still live in fixed architectural spaces. Even as we pursue diluted, fictional, movie-like spaces we spend our time in the real spaces of reality itself; even while inhaling an atmosphere suffused with technology we search for nature in the city. While pursuing tumultuous spaces of anarchic noise in which to flit about, we desire to find within them spaces of tranquillity and serenity. The more family bonds dissolve, the more people are in pursuit of home.

This dichotomy in urban life is directly analogous to a dichotomy in architecture. That is to say, the more that images of freedom are pursued in architecture, the more its conservative aspects will appear. For example, I might imagine architecture as a shelter covered with a 'single sheet of soft fabric fluttering in the wind'. I can draw this image with all the desired lightness. Then again, if I tried to execute it as an architectural project, with a physically stable structure, the various institutional constraints – functional, economic, legal – immediately raise impediments to the image of freedom. But if I try to fix this unaltered shape 'like a single sheet of fabric fluttering in the wind', it will undoubtedly become an exceedingly expressionist, awkward design. The idea of 'fabric' is just a metaphor, and we must find an architectural solution that satisfies this image.

Or when imagining an architecture that is 'as provisional as a circus tent' or 'as ephemeral as a rainbow', I'm not pursuing a mobile architecture like a real circus tent. I use these expressions in pursuit of an architecture as buoyant as a circus tent, in which the weight of its presence is not perceived.

The architectural act is always situated in the gap between this image of freedom and the institutional control of its materialisation. In the dual lifestyle compelled by the urban spaces of today, the dual character of architecture is all the more unavoidable. Architecture oscillates between illusions of freedom and the constraints of reality. However, no matter how unavoidable the constraints of reality may be, we must constantly take small steps toward liberation by depicting images of freedom. I think that future images of architecture and cities will only appear from within these attempts at liberation.

DISMANTLING AND RECONSTITUTING THE 'HOUSE' IN A DISORDERED CITY (1988)

Having been recently commissioned to design a house for a city like Tokyo, I began to ponder the question of what exactly constitutes a house. I think that residences for people leading urban lifestyles have become conclusively disengaged from reality. The kind of spaces desired in houses everywhere – a cosy living room with a low sofa facing toward audiovisual equipment, a dining room with a large table around which meals may be enjoyed, a kitchen containing splendid modular fittings – are no longer places that play a part in the simplicity and vitality of family life. Like stage-sets for television dramas, they are no more than highly fictional spaces prepared for our aspirations toward family life. In today's reality, a family restaurant probably has a greater sense of family togetherness than a dining room in a house, and the fresh food corner in a department store or a local 24-hour convenience store probably play the role of kitchen and refrigerator more than the ones in a house. Cosy, enjoyable spaces and household functions are being successively absorbed into the commercial spaces of the city. The strange vitality of Tokyo perhaps depends on the fierceness of its consumption, which now allows not only the consumption of things but also of spaces, and even of the houses that we had thought of as the final strongholds for our lives.

The central actors propelling this consumption and dismantling of houses are the women who live alone in the city. Liberated from the conventional house, they appear to succumb to the most radical and frivolous urban spaces, taking great pleasure in urban life. For them, cinemas, theatres and bars are living rooms, restaurants are dining rooms, and the pools and saunas in gyms are luxurious gardens and bathrooms. Boutique stores are their wardrobes, coin laundries their washing machines. For them, all urban spaces may be inhabited. It might even be said that the spaces connecting the trails of their behaviour constitute a house.

Do they then find the existence of a house to be no longer necessary? Has it completely dispersed into urban space? No, even for these women indulging their dreams throughout the glamorous city, there remains a 'lair' to which they should occasionally return. I have attempted to make a model house for these women: 'Pao for the Tokyo nomad girl'.

It is a temporary tent-like hut, or more precisely, a pao. Like the pao of a Mongolian nomad, it is covered with fabric, but this pao is a light, stylish membrane, as if the clothing of these women had been inflated. As is appropriate for a lair, a bed has been placed in the centre, but the periphery is defined by the three items of furniture which a nomad girl cannot be without:

1. Furniture for dressing up: a combined dresser and wardrobe. Her stage is the urban space in which she lives her dreams, and the pao is her dressing room. To behave like a beautiful star of the stage, a dressing room for the careful application of makeup and clothing is indispensable.

2. Furniture for acquiring knowledge: a desk equipped with a telephone, Walkman, mini-photo-copier, various information magazines, women's magazines and restaurant guides – an information capsule for swimming in the city, so to speak. Where to eat, what to see, where to obtain one's wardrobe – once effective information on the city comes into her hands, it can all be filed and used to define the extent of her nomadism.

3. Furniture for eating alone: a tea table for one person, combined with shelves to store a small amount of tableware. It is a small, bleak pao that awaits her descent from the stage of the city. Returning to this pao, she awakes from her dreams into a brief moment of reality. While drinking coffee alone, or occasionally eating instant noodles, she encounters periods of slight ennui.

But when the neon lights illuminate her pao in the evening, she is enlivened once more – fashionable clothes billowing in the wind, Walkman on her head, a 'Pia' [ticketing and entertainment service] in one hand, jauntily inhaling the sea of consumption.

Even if not to the same extent as the Tokyo nomad girls, our own urban lifestyles are certainly becoming increasingly nomadic. Every day, the lived experience of urban space becomes more fragmented, artificial and ephemeral. We are compelled to go back and forth between temporary, fictional urban spaces and fictional living spaces, wherein functions become the remnants of flows of images. In this lifestyle, superficial wealth and glamour are inextricably linked with an unremitting sense of emptiness.

Perhaps, however, we should now reconsider the meaning of the 'succession of temporary spaces according with events' that may be felt in this sea of consumption that mixes wealth and emptiness. There is a distinctive sense of space in Japanese cities that cannot be felt in Western cities.

In times past, when the cherry trees came into bloom, people would momentarily produce an astonishingly luxurious place for a banquet by just laying down red carpets and hanging curtains round them. A beautiful teahouse could be built by just cutting down a few trees and reassembling them. Emancipated from a finished building, a temporary space undoubtedly ensured a sensation of freedom. Perhaps within these urban spaces we may also find a truly free sense of dwelling, appropriate to our era.

TWENTY-FIRST CENTURY CURTAINS: A THEORY OF FLUID ARCHITECTURE (1990)

FROM THE SKY OVER MOROCCO

Unexpectedly, I have visited Morocco twice during the last six months. Almost 20 years had passed since I last had the opportunity to visit Casablanca and Marrakech. As I expected, Casablanca has been modernised, yet Marrakech has barely changed. In particular, the street performers that fill Djemaa el Fna square were completely unchanged, as if time had frozen. The snake charmers did the same acts, the little girls asking for money looked exactly the same. The souvenirs sold in the medina adjoining the square had not changed in the least. It is emotionally moving to be abruptly thrown from Tokyo, a city where everything changes at a dizzying rate, into a city where nothing has changed for 20 years. The amazing spaces in my memory are preserved intact in this city, and I think anyone passing through this wondrousness would find it moving.

However, during this trip I was above all moved by seeing the terrain of Morocco from the sky. When I saw the beauty of the landscape spreading below our small airplane during the two-hour round trip from Casablanca to Agadir (a resort town located on the Atlantic coast of mid-western Morocco, which is crowded with French, Spanish and other European tourists during the vacation season), I was entranced and rendered speechless.

Amid the flat farmland, like a mosaic woven from fragments of green and reddish brown, there suddenly appeared a huge, perfectly circular area of green. As we moved further away from Casablanca, the green farmland decreased and the reddish tinged earth – so red in parts that it appeared to run with blood – increased in inverse proportion. Amid this, roads delineating straight lines could sometimes be seen. Contrasting with the roads, flowing water meandered back and forth – multiple flowing lines of water completely untouched by human hand – all of them tracing sinuous curves. None progressed linearly.

It was this dynamic movement in accordance with the rhythms of nature that I found most moving. According to hydraulics researcher Theodor Schwenk (1910–1986), this meandering occurs when water flowing downstream, under the pull of gravity, encounters the eddies simultaneously engendered in the river's transverse direction. In other words, the inflected part of the flow, which is a flow through the water from inside to outside, causes a rotational movement that rises to the surface and returns to the inner part, accompanying the basic motion of the water, and this surging motion merges with the downstream motion, becoming a helical motion.[1]

Schwenk does not restrict this spiralling movement of water to merely a problem of fluids, but expands it into a fundamental principle for the morphogenesis of living things. For example, unicellular protozoa such as paramecium and stentor have spiral forms and propel themselves with a helical motion. This is because they are living things just barely differentiated from the surrounding water. Moreover, the long branching fibrous cells of algae such as spirogyras also depict spiral surfaces – shapes that visualise the motion of water itself. The winding motion of swimming water snakes, or the fanning of fish gills, are embodiments and visualisations of moving water. In short, Schwenk asserts that the structures and functions of an organism, as well as the medium surrounding that organism, all follow the same principles.[2]

Of even greater interest is his view that human tissues and organs are manifestations of the same principles. The structures of every part of a person – muscles, bone shapes, intestines, ears, throat and so on – display the imprint of the motion of flowing water. Considering the fact that during its embryonic period the physical body, floating in amniotic fluid within the womb, is almost entirely composed of water, and that even elderly people are said to be approximately 60 per cent water, I find this theory extremely compelling.

THE HUMAN BODY AS A FLUID: THE IMAGE OF VITRUVIAN MAN

Perceiving the human body as a form of movement comprising various flows, as opposed to a static and symmetrical solid, leads to a radically different worldview. In other words, according to Schwenk's theory, the parts of the human body are not just the embodiment, visualisation and solidification of flows of water, but their accumulation into a human body is also in a state of continuous transformation. This worldview distantly opposes the image of Vitruvian man, as defined in the *Ten Books of Architecture* (Book 3, Chapter 1):

Then again, in the human body the central point is naturally the navel. For if a man be placed flat on his back, with his hands and feet extended, and a pair of compasses centred at his navel, the fingers and toes of his two hands and feet will touch the circumference of a circle described therefrom. And just as the human body yields a circular outline, so too a square figure may be found from it.

It is sufficient to recall the human figure depicted by Leonardo da Vinci. The image of a man extending his robust limbs with a dignified expression is symmetrically and statically inscribed within a circle and a square. For Alberti and Da Vinci, the circle and the square are perfect geometric figures favoured by nature. Accordingly, these figures testify to the harmony and integrity of the human body and indicate a profound and essential truth about man and the world. If the ideal architectural plans of the Renaissance conformed to this ideal and immutable body figure, what kind of architecture would result from viewing the human body as a fluid? For example, what about a space enclosed only by curtains? Although curtains are today used for highly formal, ceremonial spaces, they were once used for more free and dynamic spaces unified with nature. Try to imagine a space surrounded by curtains set below cherry blossoms. People take the opportunity to gather together for the extremely ephemeral event of the blossoming of cherry trees. They choose a carpet to spread on the ground below and then, taking into account the wind and sunlight, they pull curtains around the seating area for a banquet. This is the minimum filter necessary to visualise and stabilise human actions (movements) and natural flows. It is a sign of the most primitive architectural act, that of instantaneously mediating an event integrated with nature. Furthermore, this event site is wrapped with a membrane that just barely indicates the existence of an interface.

In terms of living things, these spaces surrounded by curtains are similar to unicellular protozoa: in other words, this is just a condition in which the organisation and structure of a human body cannot yet be seen. Looking at traditional Japanese architecture, the curtain first becomes an architectural element within the stable format of a roof supported by systematically erected posts. Accordingly, while traditional architecture is oriented toward nature, it is formed in a style with a contrasting organisation and systematisation. Rather than opposing natural flows such as terrain, wind and water, it absorbs those flows, and by being closed into the minimum format of an immobile flow it is converted from an installation into architecture. Thus, white curtains billowing in the wind were incorporated in architecture as compositional elements such as *shoji* screens or *fusuma* panels. However one yields to the flows of nature, even if the flow is adopted as the form, the architecture will not become architectural unless it is constantly accompanied by actions in the opposing direction of fixity and independence. But nonetheless, we can still say this is a 180-degree shift from notions that conform to a concept of abstracted nature that entraps the human body and architecture in geometry and makes them completely independent.

ARCHITECTURE INTEGRATED
WITH THE ENVIRONMENT

The city in which I live is constantly stimulating and has provoked in me a series of architectural images. Taking a step back, the things that I build should not be described as highly creative acts, but are simply projections of various phenomena and scenes from the city, and perhaps no more than the reality of urban space viewed through a filter. So I have always thought that my architecture cannot be understood in isolation from the city.

Put another way, nature has had no impact on me at all. In my mind, nature and city, or nature and architecture, have long been antagonistic concepts. Of course, some of my architectural works have been built in natural surroundings. In such cases, I gave consideration to natural and environmental conditions such as topography, sunlight, wind direction and views. Beyond that, however, my architecture has not been actively influenced by nature. I had thought that architecture should be resolved within the autonomous system of architecture itself, and not opened up as part of a larger system that includes the environment.

However, I feel that my Guest House for Sapporo Breweries project, completed in 1989, has somewhat expanded my view on these issues. That is to say, architecture can also be viewed as, ultimately, an element in the formation of nature or the environment. Of course, it might be argued that this has been completely obvious from the outset. However, for me, the theme of how far it is possible to open up architecture has been a major issue over the decades since I began work.

Though I wouldn't go as far as calling it the wilderness of Hokkaido, the site for the Guest House for

Sapporo Breweries is a relatively large, flat field in the midst of nature. When I visited the site for the first time, in midwinter, it was blanketed with snow. The site did not contain a single tree and its boundaries were vague. This was the first time I had seen such a thing. In the city, there are always multiple regulations – site coverage ratios, floor area ratios, volumetric setbacks and so on – that almost automatically determine the appearance of the exterior form. It was obvious that all the methods I had been attempting until now would be inapplicable here. Half buried by snow, I stood stupefied.

On my way back to the city, I began to think that my only option was to bury the building underground. I thought there was no way to build a small building isolated in such a vast site. Not to mention that the architecture of thin membranes, which I had been enthusiastically describing with terms such as 'transfiguration of wind', really might be blown away by the wind. Buried underground, it would be safe, preventing the thick, heavy walls and roof from being exposed to the elements. My motives were extremely impure. Excavate the flat site, make a plaza like a buried shell, bury buildings around its perimeter, then pile up the excavated earth to make a small hill nearby.

Although my motives were impure, this 'earthwork'-like method taught me something extremely important. By manipulating the soil of this originally flat site, a topographic map of contour lines would be delineated, like a weather map indicating bands of high and low air pressure. Various flows began to occur in this terrain, like the swirling vortices of wind flows from high-pressure centres to low-pressure centres. Following these contour lines, it became possible to depict flows of people, flows of plants, flows of water. It was easy to insert the architecture within such flows. In other words, architecture was absorbed into the environment as one of its constituent elements. Rather than being an independent entity that confronts nature, architecture would become unified with nature.

The moment I began to think in this way, the assertiveness of my own architecture as a morphological expression in confrontation with the environment did not seem to be a futile gesture. Furthermore, I began to consider that this way of thinking was not limited to natural environments, and might be applied equally to an urban setting. That is to say, urban space is also nothing other than a space for flows of people, cars and various other objects. Whether one is looking at groups of buildings or plants, certain flows can be perceived, and water, air and sounds incessantly flow through all urban spaces. To make architecture in such urban spaces, the task of placing one's architecture within these relative relationships is nothing other than placing one's body within various flows.

In a city like Tokyo, even when designing a single building, the buildings surrounding the site will be completely different in terms of volume, form, number of floors, materials, structure and usage. However, one can rarely predict when each building will vanish and be replaced with a new one. Casting new architecture amid this condition is like casting pieces on a Go gameboard – a completely relative, phenomenological and playful act. This is totally different from European cities, where the act of design responds to a particular context, and gradually approaches a coherent townscape. It is an eternally repeated game. In these urban spaces, what kind of context do we have?

For these constantly changing, relativistic spaces, the only act open to us is to produce new, tense relationships. This is like the act of planting a stick in the flow of a river. The upright stick creates an eddy in the river, which interferes with other, already occurring eddies, forming a place with a more complex flow. And at the centre of these multiple small eddies is a stagnant place where people gather. This centre was once occupied by cherry blossoms or a fire. Nowadays it is probably a television or audiovisual equipment – in other words, a place where information arises. Contemporary urban space can be described as the accumulation of an incessant series of innumerable eddies.

Within these innumerable eddies we do no more than throw in new eddies in order to stimulate the environs and induce new flows in the surrounding spaces. With such a theory of relativity, perhaps we need to revise our view of our city in phenomenological terms.

In any case, the antitheses that had been troubling me – the oppositions between city and nature, or architecture and nature – began gradually to dissolve. Intently thinking about how to open my architecture over the preceding decades, I concluded that architecture should be absorbed into the environment.

TWENTY-FIRST CENTURY CURTAINS

My project for a 'Media Ship Floating on the Seine River' (Franco-Japanese Cultural Centre competition entry) is a proposal for a phenomenological, relativistic architecture for the media era. The core of this project is formed by three media ships, that is to say, information-emitting devices. These media ships float in the air and are reflected in the Seine, which flows in front of the site. They transmit a variety of information to the surrounding areas. In accordance with the character of the information, the periphery is divided into spaces with different functions, such as a theatre, an art gallery, a café, a library and a seminar space. In order to isolate each separate space, corrugated screens are placed to enclose each information source. Much as curtains did in the past, these screens serve as lightweight partitions that just barely define fields where people may gather.

In addition, a glass screen stands along the street frontage to isolate the entire building from the outer world. This screen is also intended to be the thinnest possible isolating membrane, an interface with the environment like a curtain for a field where people may gather. Comprising a sandwich panel of liquid crystal and glass, the transparency and opacity of each delicate panel can be controlled electronically. In other words, like a large electronic scoreboard, it is possible to freely depict a pattern using the transparency and opacity of every part of the facade.

This general area is strongly influenced by one of Paris's urban axes, and architectural elements such as the corrugated screens and media ships are organised and structured by inserting a grid frame parallel or perpendicular to this axis line.

Thus the media ships take the place of cherry blossoms (information), and the screens with inserted liquid crystal can be regarded as curtains for the twenty-first century, supported by new technologies. These curtains can be opaque, as if clouds or fog had appeared, or transparent, as if they had cleared. The backdrop comprises the solid volumes located along the Paris axis, their visibility changing according to the level of transparency required. Concealing the activities and following the incessant flows of nature and information, the various eddies produced inside are wrapped with a light membrane, and an architecture of minimal forms is arranged between them – this is the 'Media Ship Floating on the Seine River' concept.

As I have already mentioned, people once placed their bodies within the restlessly changing flows of nature, giving it a barely permanent form and creating an open architectural style. Today we place our bodies not only within nature but within the still more dynamic flows of the city. In these unstable, transient, phenomenological and relativistic spaces, we must also find the minimum fixed system and convert phenomenal spaces into durable architecture. Furthermore, it is impossible for today's architecture to avoid a connection with the tremendous energy of consumer society and the accelerating speed of transformation of the environment. Wherever we look, we cannot find a stable foundation for architecture. Architecture that yields to the flows and only pursues phenomena will surely be immediately consumed. However, architecture that ponderously settles into place by just relying on the appearance of clichéd architectural formats has absolutely no resonance with the era. Overflowing with vitality, the architecture of today can just barely exist in the contradiction between the unstable condition of ceaseless flows and the stable systems shared by people.

Due to the remarkably limited sightlines facing the narrow stage in Nō theatre – said to be the most accomplished performance art style – the body of an actor may display a 'posture of suspense'.[3] The upper body leans forward from the seat and, as if drawn upward, the chest of this leaning upper body will again bulge. It is said that in order to prepare this body posture, unstable energy is first produced within the body. Thus, Nō dance is not simply walking on a stage, but inducing energy produced by the body posture, then moving to the place led by the energy. The performance becomes 'fluid energy'.[4]

This observation is extremely evocative. How can we derive fluid energy from an unstable posture on a stage? The architecture of today is that which a superb Nō actor can convey with nothing more than their body language.

NOTES

1. Theodor Schwenk, *Sensitive Chaos: The Creation of Flowing Forms in Water and Air*, translated by Olive Whicher and Johanna Weigley (London: Rudolf Steiner Press, 1965).

2. Ibid.

3. Keiichiro Tsuchiya, *Nō* (Tokyo: Shinyosha, 1989).

4. Ibid.

ARCHITECTURE FOR
THE SIMULATED CITY
(1991)

Map-like aerial images of Tokyo flow across the floor.
Photographs taken automatically from an altitude of 300m
are graphically processed by computer and smoothly homogenised. Alternatively, the backs of the heads of young
boys facing game machines in a video arcade are aligned
on the screens. The images then instantaneously change
to a scene of an expressway taken from a video game.
The scenery vanishes at the speed of Akira racing on his
motorcycle in the eponymous movie. Even here, the sense
of depth on the screens is completely erased by graphic
processing and transformed into cartoon landscapes.

A 10m-wide and 28m-long floating floor has been
paved with translucent acrylic panels. An undulating
5m-high translucent acrylic screen has been set
horizontally; one part of this incorporates a liquid-crystal
sheet, the transparency of which can be electronically
controlled. Another wall is clad with aluminium panels;
perpendicular to it, a translucent cloth hangs from the
ceiling. All these elements are screens for images from
44 projectors. Eighteen projectors are suspended from the
ceiling, and shine images on the acrylic floor, while the
remaining 26 units shine overlapping images from behind
hanging acrylic or fabric screens.

Numerous images have been edited and collected on
12 laser discs. These are mostly scenes of everyday life in
Tokyo. Crowds of people traverse zebra crossings,
businessmen converse on the railway platform while
waiting for a train, young people talk on public telephones,
and so on. These incessantly changing video images are

collaged on 44 screens. The images are mostly random, but occasionally all 44 screens show the same image. Ambient sounds processed by a synthesiser are emitted from 16-channel speakers, making the space more three-dimensional.

Titled 'Dreams', this space was the third room of the *Visions of Japan* exhibition, held in London. Visitors at the show were inundated with floating video images and saturated with sounds. Their bodies floated on the river of the acrylic floor and swayed as if they were seasick. Crown Prince Hironomiya of Japan, attending the opening of the show, said he was sure he would have felt the space more intensely if he had drunk alcohol beforehand. Prince Charles, on the other hand, asked me what lay beyond the images. I answered that there might be nothing beyond them, and so he asked if I was an optimist. I answered that of course I was.

According to exhibition producer Arata Isozaki, the space was originally to have been titled 'Simulations': it was renamed 'Dreams' in response to opinions from the London side that 'Simulations' would be too obscure for ordinary museum visitors. Yet the space is an accurate simulation of the reality of Tokyo, or perhaps it is more accurate to say that Tokyo is a simulated city. For instance, the experience of walking through the Kabuki-cho district at night closely resembles the experience of this imagistic space. In either space, our bodies float amid vast images and showers of sounds. When gazing into video-game screens, we are already on the other side of the screens. As suggested by Crown Prince Hironomiya, we become intoxicated by the spatial illusions of light and sound, and as implied by Prince Charles, we are paused in a space without hope. Perhaps we will never arrive in either future.

There exists, however, one distinct difference between the 'Simulations' room and the reality of Kabuki-cho. Compared to the real Kabuki-cho, which brims with noise and chaos, the city collages projected on the screens are suffused with white noise. Or, they merge into streams of computer graphics that represent physical flows. In other words, the urban scenes lose their distinct outlines and dissolve into morning haze. All the scenes of reality merge into a state of calm oblivion that may be called 'nirvana'. If we are to imagine the future, what else can we expect but a state of extreme technological control?

Five objects were placed within the deluge of images in this space. Designed by Anthony Dunne, a young British designer, these objects could be described as television sets fresh out of their packages, or as comical androids inhaling the atmosphere of information. In any case, they are objects that generate weird sounds and transform images in response to the noises suffusing this atmosphere. They use readymade containers, but in comparison to commercially available television sets, which unidirectionally absorb the major flows of information, these are personal, poetic objects that allow us to recognise anew that our surroundings are suffused with noise. Perhaps somewhere inside our bodies we have already begun to grow an additional organ that inhales noises in the same way as these objects. Even if we cannot visualise it, our bodies are unceasingly touching and sensing this atmosphere of technology, which forms our bodily rhythms. As each day passes, we may have already begun to possess an android-like body without our being aware of it.

Okawabata River City 21 Main Gate, known as the 'Egg of Winds', was based on a very similar concept. Wrapped with aluminium panels, an egg with a maximum length of about 16m and a maximum diameter of 8m floats in front of two high-rise apartment buildings. During the day, the egg is merely an object reflecting sunlight, but at night five LCD projectors installed inside the egg are switched on. They project images from videotapes and television onto the partly perforated aluminium-panelled exterior surface and directly onto the screens inside. The aluminium egg has a silver gleam in daytime, but when night falls, it transforms into a hologram-like presence, a sculpture comprising nothing but vague three-dimensional images without a sense of reality. People on the street look up at the egg, pause and suspiciously mutter, 'what's that?', before moving on. The object is not a street-side television, and it differs in character from the Jumbotrons that decorate the facades of railway station buildings. It is an image object that becomes visible due to the information-suffused surrounding atmosphere. It is an image object that appears and disappears with the wind.

During the same period that I built the 'Egg of Winds' a model with a very similar shape was displayed at an exhibition venue in Brussels. To be honest, this was the initial model for the River City 21 Gate – that is to say, a model formed as a ship-like polyhedron comprising triangular planes. The Brussels 'Egg of Winds' was wrapped with translucent fabric and perforated aluminium panels, and also had a floor made of translucent acrylic. Though people could not enter, they could still look into the translucent egg and see chairs and tables made of translucent materials, lit by natural light from above. In short, people could see the illusion of a packaged urban lifestyle in the egg. These were all temporary and insub-stantial objects, like a mirage. Rather than possessing structure, they resembled ephemeral natural phenomena, sometimes appearing and sometimes disappearing in the atmosphere, like rainbows.

Accordingly, if these two Eggs of Winds are superim-posed, they could almost be described as the 'design of atmosphere'. If some kind of spray were to be dispersed into this atmosphere filled with as yet unvisualised information, image-like objects might faintly appear. The act of making architecture today might be described as the discovery of such sprays, that is to say, filters that enable visualisation.

In this sense the Tower of Winds, built some years ago in front of Yokohama Station, could be said to best embody the 'design of atmosphere'. The tower's distin-guishing characteristic is that it is an object of light deliber-ately placed in an environment surrounded by neon lights – not an artwork placed in a museum. While in terms of spectacle the tower cannot compete with the neon lights in the vicinity, it uses almost the same blinking rhythm, so people are engulfed by the impression that the atmosphere in the vicinity of the tower is being distilled. My intention was not for light to be emitted from a material object set in the atmosphere, but for the atmosphere itself to be converted into light.

The River City 21 Egg of Winds was initially intended to engender a future house, that is to say, it was to be an image for a new dwelling model. It cost so much to create the shell alone that the image could not be realised; still, what should be discernible in the original atmosphere is a new lifestyle for a simulated city. On the other hand, the Brussels 'Egg of Winds' is also named 'Pao for the Tokyo Nomad Girl', which was for me the image model for an urban dwelling. Parallel to the increasingly imagistic quality of urban lifestyles, it depicted an image of an urban lifestyle that departs from reality as the days go by. Therefore, the attribute common to both eggs is that they are containers suggestive of new lifestyles. In short, I wanted to indicate here that the loss of reality in urban lifestyles has a complementary relationship with this image-like architecture.

In every era, dreams of new lifestyles lead to the emergence of new spaces. For instance, the dreams of 'modern living' given to people in the 1950s were spatially materialised in images of a bright, electrified lifestyle. Well-lit houses with large openings, sheltered by flat roofs or very low-pitched roofs, industrialised kitchens with built-in refrigerators and gas stoves, dining chairs with chrome-plated pipe frames and thin bent ply backs – these bright images promoted a modernised lifestyle focused on the nuclear family. Wearing a clean white shirt, the father works in a bright steel-and-glass office building and comes home to his smiling wife and children waiting in an electrified kitchen and dining room. The picture is completed by a Volkswagen Beetle or a Citroen 2CV parked in the garage.

If the ideal lifestyle for the electric age was spatialised as this kind of modern living, we have not yet found spaces appropriate to the ideal lifestyle of the computer age. Rather than houses, the recent situation is best symbolised by the differences between the Volkswagens and Citroen 2CVs of former times and the Toyotas and Nissans of today. That is to say, as opposed to the Volkswagens and Citroen 2CVs, which were designed with forms directly alluding to the functions of their various mechanisms, today's Japanese cars are entirely wrapped in smooth, superficial designs that conceal the technology – the intelligent electronics – inside. Today's cars are based on image designs that are mostly unrelated to their internal workings. Various other household electric appliances could be described as following almost the same design concept.

Just as automotive design and industrial design have adapted to consumer needs – in other words, to fashionable modern styles – we can see the same increasing superficiality in the case of dwellings, though here the designs are solely oriented toward conservatism. In the world of architecture, where functions and forms have never been strictly related, styles tend to express a nostalgic longing for an economically stable lifestyle.

However, what actually constitutes the new lifestyle of today? It seems this is a question we are too busy to think about, distracted as we are by the constant parade of gorgeous new items and spaces. The multiple foodstuffs, items of clothing and daily necessities that we see glittering on the shelves of department stores and convenience stores promise to fulfil our dreams of a new lifestyle. But the moment we eat, wear or place them in our dwellings, they lose their lustre, and we have to start our pursuit of novelty all over again.

From daily necessities to houses, products that may superficially appear quite individualistic in fact conceal a homogenisation that increases day by day. Conversely, as symbolised by contemporary automotive design, it is the homogeneity of their contents that sustains the individuality of their outward appearance (albeit with slight variations). Not just houses but larger works of architecture are heading for the same fate. For example, the development of air-conditioning technology isolates architecture from local climates, ensuring that architecture of the same style is possible anywhere in the world. Moreover, any style of architecture may be supported. Even the apparently rich individuality of the multiple works of architecture in our surroundings is, in many cases, no more than the superficial decoration of homogeneous content with differing forms. These buildings are like the perishable, Saran-wrapped goods that you see in the windows of convenience stores. A display of such rich variety is only possible by covering it with Saran wrap, freezing it, and placing it in a homogeneous state.

Since the emergence of steel and glass, we have been in pursuit of the homogeneity known as 'universal space'. However, this universal space, like the coordinate axes of Euclidean geometry itself, may be rationally homogeneous but finally does not quite attain homogeneity. Rather, the tendency to express regionalism in architecture, and the desire for a strong sense of monumentality, could perhaps be said to have prevented neutral homogenisation.

The phenomenon of homogenisation in today's architectural space could therefore be said to have a very different appearance from the former aesthetic pursuit of universal space. What is being homogenised today is society itself, and for architects to oppose this is futile. The more that architects rely on individual – or rather, personal – expression, the more they fall into a homogeneity that just connects points on the coordinate axes of Euclidean geometry. The whole of society is becoming enveloped with a large sheet of Saran wrap.

Architects used to yearn for homogeneous grids because society was assumed to be opaque. They attempted to incorporate transparent, neutral grids into a society that seemed as opaque and heterogeneous as lava. Consequently, even if homogenisation was achieved in a universal office space, this was an experiment within a closed field. If they took one step outside of the office, they found real, opaque spaces.

Today, our environment is suffused with a vacant brightness. Just like the commodities crammed on convenience store shelves, our cities have become desiccated and bleak. Over the last ten years, moisture has been removed from cities, as if they had been thrown into a huge tumble drier. While surrounded with a variety of goods, we are living within utter homogeneity. Our affluence is supported by a sheet of Saran wrap.

The formation of a simulated lifestyle is predicated on the Saran wrap that envelops society. For instance, rather than going directly home at the end of the day, businessmen and office ladies will stop off downtown. There they drink, eat, sing, dance, talk. Sometimes they amuse themselves at the cinema or theatre, play video games, or go shopping. Swim or run at a sports club. The times and spaces that belong to the interval between office and home are, for them, completely fictional. They eat and drink as if it were their own mothers' cooking, sing and dance as if they were celebrities, converse drunkenly as if with their closest friends, purchase their dreams of affluence, exercise in artificial spaces as if they were swimming in the sea and running around a field. Each of these spaces, actions and even the objects acquired in this intermediate zone, are all simulations. Moreover, these simulated lifestyles and spaces, no longer confined to the intermediate zone of downtown, have infiltrated offices and houses. Our entire lifestyle, including family and work, is now simulated. The distinction between real and unreal has been lost.

Needless to say, from our sense of sight through to taste, hearing and touch, we have lost our sense of reality. We have completely lost our sense of conviction about what is truly delicious, what we are actually hearing, what we are really touching. That is because our body itself undergoes transformation without relation to our consciousness. Or because our mutual communication systems have undergone radical changes. We have been provided with bodies that may easily invert the relationship between reality and unreality by the single movement of an image.

The growth of media has detached words from things, and diluted the reality of the things themselves. By means of words and pictures alone, unaccompanied by things, we are increasing the proliferation of images. Thus, a simulated lifestyle expands our own selves into other fields. Communication through media – that is to say, communication unaccompanied by physical substance – has become normal for us, and unmediated communications finally have become ineffective. The old communication networks, rooted in regions and places, have become almost meaningless. Under the abnormal influence of dwelling in cities, this could be described as the negation of physical distances due to the increase of an instantaneous, temporary network formed by innumerable types of media.

Thus, when building architecture for a simulated city, we must answer two difficult questions. One is the question of how to make substantial architecture while substantial things are losing their meaning, and the other is the question of how we can build enduring architecture within the process of regional communities being negated as media communication networks appear and disappear, disappear and appear.

These two questions are truly perplexing. Both are contradictory conditions. What kind of architecture is possible within such contradictory relationships?

Of course, there may be no definitive solutions for such abstruse questions. What is clear, however, is that it is meaningless for us to stand outside and view a contradictory place as non-contradictory, that is to say, to not acknowledge the contradiction. All that remains for us is to close the gaps in these contradictions as best we can. That is to say, the first problem is how to make fictional architecture or imagistic architecture, and the second problem is how to make ephemeral architecture or temporary architecture. These adjectives do not mean that architecture should be replaced with images, or that temporary things should be used as architecture. Rather, we must build imagistic (fictional) and temporary (ephemeral) entities as permanent architecture. Today, when all of society is wrapped in a large sheet of Saran wrap, it is impossible for us to make foodstuffs covered in Saran wrap appear to be the genuine article. We can, however, beautifully visualise the Saran wrap itself. I think that the future of architecture now depends on how we reveal the structures of these fictions.

ARCHITECTURAL SCENERY IN THE SARAN WRAP CITY (1992)

Recently, for the first time in three years, I saw the waterfront of Tokyo Bay from a ship. Every time I come here, I'm seized by deep, inexpressible emotions as I catch glimpses of an aspect of Tokyo's grandeur that remains unseen when one is inside the city: the innumerable clusters of shipping containers sliding down unmanned conveyor belts, the incredible mountains of garbage piling up, the many and varied vessels plying the polluted sea. Rather than a waterfront, I comprehend this as the backyard of a huge metropolis. Inside it every day, I experience nothing but spaces of dazzling fictions, but when seen as if from backstage, the vast quantities of energy and machinery, and the real spaces that support these fictions, are made visible.

However, the waterfront has undergone great changes in a mere three years. This backdrop to the huge alien life-form that is the city – that is to say, the bay area on its outer edge – is imperceptibly transforming into a new interior. The waterfront from Shinagawa to Harumi is lined with huge numbers of skyscrapers, highways stretch over the sea to connect the landward side to the reclaimed land of Ariake, while the artificial islands adjacent to Yumenoshima are linked to the existing city by a multitude of pipelines and densely packed with an unbelievable number of cranes.

Standing on top of the 120m-high abutment of the crossing bridge, I am lost for words at the immensity of the energy concentrated in this constantly reborn city. I'm just stupefied. Any sentiment for history is utterly crushed.

Perhaps within a few years dozens of skyscrapers will have arisen on these artificial islands, and surely urban activities will then commence. It's like an efficient artificial organ connected to the alien.

Utterly new kinds of urban spaces are constantly emerging here, of a kind we have never before experienced. Groups of buildings are erected on arid, homogeneous plots of land. They are completely detached from their *genius loci*. To be sure, architecture estranged from the land can still be impressive. Cities unburdened by history, such as Houston and Atlanta, are not uncommon. Tsukuba University Town and Tama New Town are highly artificial constructions. However, given the ferocious speed of construction with which crisp-edged plots of land continue to suddenly appear in the sea, this waterfront is dominated by an unprecedented and strange homogeneity. By comparison, even the business district near the west exit of Shinjuku Station, crowded with uniform skyscrapers, is a serene and sentimental scene.

If architecture has become estranged from the land, can the field of architecture itself truly survive? When thinking about the homogeneity that pervades Tokyo, our insistence on the specialised logic of architecture begins to seem pointless, even without witnessing stupefying scenes like those on the waterfront.

More than being difficult to resist, it's a pleasant feeling of being detached from your own body. This vast, homogeneous space pervading Tokyo is not so old. It probably goes back only a few years, or about ten years at the most.

Since entering the 1980s, we have begun to live in two cities. One is the city-as-substance, a city supported by physical existence and objects, and with which we have been intimately accustomed since ancient times. It has a spatial hierarchy that corresponds to the social organisation of individual–family–regional community–nation. Accordingly, it's a city with a network system that extends in concentric circles, and provides a static, stable order. All modern urban planning theories seem to have been predicated on the notion of the city-as-substance.

By contrast, the city-as-phenomenon appeared after 1980, together with the sudden development of a society permeated by electronic media. This is the city as information, the virtual city as event. Without the stable spatial and temporal order of the city-as-substance, it's a city without hierarchy that extends topologically in space and time.

These two cities have arisen like the two sides of the same coin, and needless to say they cannot be clearly separated. However, the city-as-phenomenon kept expanding throughout the 1980s, and gradually began to form unique spaces independent of the city-as-substance. While this is by no means limited to the city, in a developed consumerist society it occurs parallel to the way signs are inevitably detached from substance and become phenomena that can walk on their own two legs. Put conversely, we consume only signs and progressively discard the objects themselves, and finally even begin to apply such consumerist society mechanisms to architecture and urban space. As a result, the built surfaces that cover the city are clad with innumerable ornaments, and architecture-as-substance is hidden. Not limited to the neon lights and various signboards and show-windows of commercial architecture, this applies to the brazen, luxurious expressions of entire facades. This phenomenon is also obvious in the commodified houses made by kitset housemaker companies, even if their exteriors may look stylish. So in the afternoon, all these urban spaces are like places for storing bulky garbage, but from evening onward, they change radically and into scenes that make you wonder if you are standing within a kaleidoscopic interior. The thickness and weight of the object-as-substance is diluted, and the most enchanting moment for a city like Tokyo is in the evening time when urban spaces composed only of phenomena of light and image begin to appear. This is a moment in which the body becomes intoxicated by the city-as-phenomena, and dissolves. The body that should have resisted being consumed is now swallowed by a city that is like an alien without substance.

The city-as-phenomenon is timeless and placeless. Such urban spaces can be characterised by the five words homogeneity, transparency, liquidity, relativity and fragmentation. We arrive at a space that is neutral, unambiguous, dry, odourless and homogeneous. A rarefied, transparent space in which the thickness and weight of objects cannot be felt. A transient space of ceaseless flow in which each sign gives rise to the next sign. A relative space that prepares alternatives able to be copied at any time, a fragmentary space unable to attain a spatially and temporally closed cosmos.

We can see the apotheosis of such spaces in the typical convenience store. The shelves are inundated by every possible lifestyle commodity, with no hierarchy among them. All the commodities are set parallel. They aren't gaudily decorated, and the distinctions between high-level goods and cheap items are relativised only by simple differences in cost. Perishable foods are covered with Saran wrap, and thereby homogenised and relativised. By being wrapped with sheets of thin, transparent film, all perishable foodstuffs are deprived of any sense of vitality, and take on a neutral, abstract, symbolic existence. Rather than its original function of preserving freshness, the primary role of the transparent film is to ensure a homogeneity that guarantees the ability to make a fair selection.

However, the characteristics of homogeneity, transparency and liquidity that seem to pervade the real city are all attributes that were pursued in the modern architecture of the early twentieth century. For instance, homogeneity is symbolically expressed in Mies van der Rohe's concepts of universal space and the aesthetic of 'less is more'. These were spatially embodied by the neutral grid of the steel frame. Transparency was an extremely important term, as demonstrated in the concepts behind the early works of Walter Gropius and Le Corbusier. According to Colin Rowe, analogies may be made between their buildings and the paintings of László Moholy-Nagy and Fernand Léger. Liquidity was candidly expressed in Giedion's concepts of space–time and the mutual interpenetration of interior and exterior space. Moreover, relativity and fragmentation routinely appeared in the collage techniques of the Russian avant-garde. In short, these keywords indicate the fundamental aesthetic concepts that wrap modernist architecture and art.

In this sense, it might be said that the modernist aesthetic has been fully realised in urban spaces based on consumerism. To be sure, rather than being a world of individual architectural and artistic expressions, our city is collectively far more homogeneous, transparent, fluid, relative and fragmentary. A neutral and invisible grid seems to extend infinitely throughout our surroundings. All personal, phenomenological expressions can be seen as the play of transparent signs within these coordinate axes. No matter how much individual works of architecture attempt to assert their originality, the instant they are placed in the city, they start to look like the food items covered with Saran wrap arrayed in the windows of convenience stores. Put conversely, all personal, phenomenological expressions are given the possibility of implementation by being covered in Saran wrap. Without the Saran wrap, homogeneity and transparency cannot be preserved in this city.

Originally the steel and glass, or pure-white cubes, of Mies and Corbu were inserted into Europe's cities of stone and brick – in other words, into the spaces of an opaque, heterogeneous and extremely substantial city. However, the circumstances are now completely reversed: the spaces in which these structures are grounded are shrouded in transparency and homogeneity. What kind of architecture can we embed in such ground? Are all our attempts enabled by the presence of Saran wrap? Without the persistent presence of this transparent film, it's impossible to ascertain the domain of architecture within this city.

In contrast with the attempts of the city-as-substance to preserve regional communities, the city-as-phenomenon nullifies the tyranny of the former through media. Moreover, in the city-as-substance, the house expresses a closed cosmology. In the spaces of a house, the relationships between individual–family–society are explicitly replaced by diagrams of private room–living room, or the route from dining room–entry hall. The centre of the domestic spaces is composed of the living and dining rooms, expressing a strongly centripetal form with regard to the exterior. The private rooms are peripheral spaces enclosing this strong centre.

However, in the city-as-phenomenon, rather than confronting the family, individual family members confront society through media and multiple interlaced networks. Particularly with the telephone, communications expand so as to transcend time and space, followed by diverse transportation networks. Individuals are tied to each other through innumerable tree-shaped networks. Individuals turn their faces directly and completely toward society, and faces that are turned toward the family become secondary. The compositions of conventional domestic spaces now give rise to large disjunctions with reality. A planning layout in which each private room in a dwelling directly confronts society, while the living and dining rooms exist behind them as optional spaces, seems much closer to real lifestyles. At this moment, the centrality of the house is demolished, and simultaneously the cosmology of the house too. A dwelling cannot avoid being transformed into flat and homogeneous spaces.

But in order to maintain the system in which the family unit is the most important unit of society – whatever the degree of its collapse – the cosmologically complete dwelling will not vanish. To the extent that individuals directly confront society, the living and dining spaces must be kept as simulated spaces that symbolise a pseudo-family. The diagram of the confrontation between decorative, stylish detached houses and one-room apartments in residential areas graphically reveals the hidden conflict between these pseudo-cosmological spaces and those isolated individual spaces that have lost their sense of community.

Enormous commercial complexes provide places for face-to-face communication among those innumerable contingent groups that are conspicuous throughout the city. They fragment and manifest the functions that formerly were found inside the house, dispersing them throughout the city. Cafés, bars and restaurants stand in for living and dining rooms, 24-hour convenience stores for refrigerators, boutiques for wardrobes, gymnasiums for vast gardens, fast-food chains for kitchens, and so on. While honing their infinitesimal differences, each space summons people across time and distance, providing extremely ephemeral and accidental community spaces. Similar to the way that the living and dining rooms inside a dwelling function as simulated spaces for a family, the huge commercial spaces in the city are fragments of the simulated spaces of a dwelling. The spaces that act as the nuclei of dwellings and regional communities continue to be nullified by these simulated spaces covered in Saran wrap. Urban lifestyles are unilaterally compelled to become simulated. As a result, in the city-as-substance we carry on living in permanent residences that are unchanged from the past, while in the city-as-phenomenon we are nomads assembling a virtual house by linking simulated spaces. The nomadic lifestyle is possible only in a city covered with Saran wrap, and the moment it is removed, we will settle in a permanent place. The nomads of the Saran wrap city are sustained by such a double life.

The body-as-consciousness can live in the virtual city-as-phenomenon, whereas the physical body cannot transcend time and distance. In the same way, architecture-as-image can exist in the city-as-phenomenon, whereas architecture-as-substance cannot exceed space or time. Just as the physical body is unable to completely unify its lives in these two different cities, architecture is also unable to support this contradiction: it may have become estranged from its land, but as a physical presence it cannot detach itself from the earth and float about in space. The result is that, while architecture is no more than an exterior surface decorated with facile, gaudy symbols, the backdrop remains the same old kind of solemn substance. Architecture in the Saran wrap city doesn't seem to lean in either direction. That is to say, it can't be biased to the indulgent, temporary symbolic expressions enabled by the Saran wrap, and neither can it insist on the presence of only those things that have discarded the Saran wrap. To the extent that the two cities in which we live form two sides of the same coin, we live in these two cities simultaneously, and it's impossible to abstract just one of them. In this sense, the architecture we now pursue is nothing other than a manifestation of the Saran wrap.

To manifest the Saran wrap – in other words, to give that transparent film a structure – is to produce a 'device that generates phenomena'. It doesn't exist as phenomena itself; it is a substance that produces and enables phenomena. It is a device that generates landscape, a device that visualises the flows of invisible things like air, and a device that hints at human activity (communications) – that is to say, architecture as a device that generates programming. Though I call it a device, it has a completely different topology from the morphological analogy of the machine pursued by modernism at the beginning of the twentieth century. Rather, it is like a 'barcode', completely without formal expression itself; while an extremely simple substance, it is architecture as a system that triggers diverse meanings. I can't seem to stop myself from coming up with new keywords, but the architecture of the Saran wrap city might also be called 'barcode architecture'.

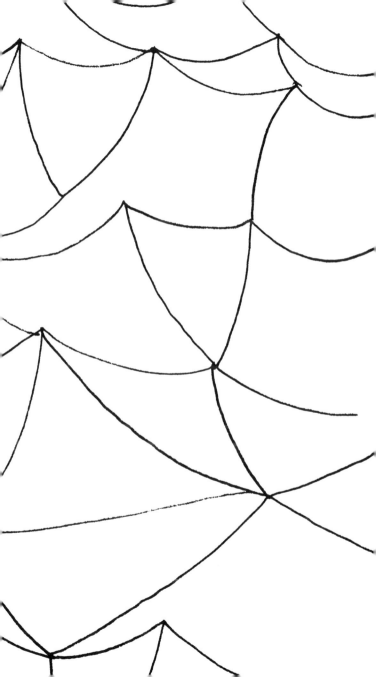

A GARDEN OF MICROCHIPS
(1993)

THE VISUAL IMAGE IN THE
ERA OF MICROELECTRONICS

I believe that the 1990 exhibition *Information Art – The Diagramming of Microchips*, held at the Museum of Modern Art (MoMA) in New York, was an event of great importance for the world of architecture and design. I did not see the exhibition but, judging by the catalogue, it consisted of numerous photographs of microchips blown up hundreds of times, in other words diagrammatic images of the integrated circuits used in computers.

The microchips look like delicately woven textiles, made up of patterns of bright colours applied to the silicon in such a way as to form grids. Each image, however, is different from the others. In some striped patterns are repeated, while in others they are subdivided into a patchwork of blocks of different patterns and colours. Many chips have borders and are composed of cell-like squares, arranged like the representation of buildings in a plan. One shows a complex diagram with a pattern that is reminiscent of an organic form, looking like the nervous system of the human body superimposed on a chequerboard.

In any case, the patterns of microchips are electronic textiles that suggest the image of the plan of a contemporary city. A chip, so small that it has to be enlarged hundreds of times before it is visible to the naked eye, can contain millions and, more recently, tens of millions of transistors. Currently, a chip containing billions of them is under development. In addition, the patterns that look like flat surfaces are in reality three-dimensional structures made up of anything from 10 to 25 layers.

The exhibition at MoMA seemed truly innovative to me because the photographs of microchips were used to make the aesthetics of the era of microelectronics visible in images. It succeeded in giving form, for the first time in a decisive manner, to the image of a new aesthetics that is replacing the dominant machine-age aesthetic of the twentieth century.

Almost 50 years have passed since the invention of the transistor and as far back as the 1960s the computer had already made surprising progress. You will probably be asking why it is only now that I am referring to the microelectronic era, given that the transition from mechanics to electronics occurred a long time ago. It is true that even at the time of the Tokyo Olympics, the booking system for the Shinkansen bullet train showed us that computer technology was going to modify society in an irreversible way.

And yet, despite the fact that microelectronics had made amazing progress, we had not yet succeeded in moulding it into clear visible images, as had been done for the machine age. In the field of architecture and design, however much effort we made to imagine the society of the future, we continued to be dependent on visual forms of expression. This difficulty was evident in the images of the city and the works of architecture produced in rapid succession by the Archigram group, which so fascinated young architects and students in the 1960s. Projects like Peter Cook's Plug-in City (1964) and Instant City (1969) and Ron Herron's Walking City (1964) represented visualisations of a technological utopia arising out of a system made up of the machine and the human being playing with the computer.

Although extraordinary imagination went into their design, these cities of the future remained within the aesthetic realm of the machine. They were collages of mechanical objects like huge cranes, three-dimensional structures, launch ramps for missiles and space shuttles on their way to the Moon. Looking back at these projects, only the one called Computer City (1964) by Dennis

Crompton traced the image of a network, a grid, resembling the nervous system. Nevertheless, even this project seems to be a substitute for an integrated circuit, enlarged and configured as the layout of a city plan. In other words, the structure of the city is once again determined by a simple visual analogy. It is precisely at this point that we discover the reason why it is almost impossible to outline the aesthetics of the era of microelectronics. Whereas in the machine era aircraft, ships, cars and their mechanical components such as motors, screws and hubs in and of themselves constituted an image of the age, in the electronic era we have not yet found a visual form that can produce a representative iconography.

The form of mechanical objects expresses some sort of causal relationship, however ambiguous, with their function. In the case of vehicles, a dynamic form that opposes less resistance to the air or water results in greater speed. The myth that the best form is the one that most closely matches function dominated the world of design throughout the twentieth century. In the case of electronic objects, on the other hand, there is no causal relationship between function and form. Even in objects that generate images or sounds, such as audiovisual devices, form does not follow function. The enormous memory and calculation capacities of the computer conjure up no formal image. All that appears before our eyes are the data to be entered and the results obtained. We cannot even imagine the electric current, its speed and its huge volume. It is for this reason that, in order to 'see' the image of the electronic age, we have started to use the image of mechanical objects as a surrogate. Yet microchips set out in this way clearly suggest images totally different from those of mechanical objects. Such images are not so much forms as spaces in which invisible things flow. It could be said that what we are dealing with here is a transparent space in which, as soon as the flow is produced, different phenomenological forms emerge. It seems, in this case, that the visualisation of the image of a space that generates expressions is more important than the forms expressed.

It is often claimed that the design of new cars in our country is a product of the electronic era and does not express an immediately recognisable, solid form, as in the case of such celebrated European cars as the Porsche or Mercedes-Benz. Japanese cars are delicate and present an image as subtle and elusive as mist. Their speed is not necessarily translated into an aerodynamic form; on the contrary, one has the impression that they have been designed to circulate silently in a world with no air. At the base of such vehicles must lie the electronic and transparent pace symbolised by the microchip. Does that not mean that forms as subtle and elusive as mist are fragments of phenomenological design, images that are born and vanish in the middle of that space?

THE CITY IS A GARDEN OF MICROCHIPS

The blown-up diagram of a microchip looks like an aerial photograph of a city, processed on the computer. If transformed by means of an effector, the photograph of an urban area can become an abstract diagram that shows only the empty outline of the buildings and the works of civil engineering, filled with luminous and coloured points. The real appearance of urban space is cancelled out and the image starts to resemble a photograph of a microchip.

A symbolic value attaches to the fact that as soon as the substance of urban space is eliminated another city emerges: the city as microchip. In that moment the city is not just diagrammatically analogous to the microchip, but even begins to display similar characteristics, which can be summed up by three terms: fluidity, multiplicity of layers, phenomenality. I have already pointed out on several occasions that urban space is made up of immovable objects like buildings and works of civil engineering, and is at the same time an accumulation of various elements that flow. These flows are generated by a range of different forces such as water and wind or people and cars, as well as by different types of energy and information.

Originally Japanese cities developed by exploiting the variety of the natural terrain, shaped by the topography of the ground and the action of rivers and other currents of water, and then overlaid with the networks of roads and canals constructed by human beings. At Edo [the old name of the city of Tokyo] in particular, an interesting urban space was created, where natural variations of relief, roads and canals were fused in a harmonious way. Looking at the *Bushu Toyoshima-gun Edo Shozu,* considered the oldest surviving map of Edo and representing the city as it was around the middle of the seventeenth century, what we see is a network of rivers, roads and canals that extend outwards in spirals from Edo Castle as if in a dynamic configuration. Here we see clearly how the pattern, which in theory should have been traced by the roads, is twisted and bent under the influence of the spiral configuration of the different undulating lines and transformed into a profoundly organic and fluid space. The space formed is totally different from the Western one, in which geometric patterns are imposed in a rigorous fashion on the natural relief, even though based on it. In the *Edo ikkenzu byobu* [a screen with a panoramic view of Edo], which is thought to have been painted at the beginning of the nineteenth century by Esaitsuguzane Kuwagata, the spiral configuration of the place is even clearer. The picture is a view from above, looking in the direction of Edo Castle and Mount Fuji, painted from the highest point of the Fukagawa district. In it we see groups of houses, corresponding to the residences of feudal lords and the homes of ordinary people, which form undulating lines along the watercourses and the areas of greenery. And it is clear that at that time there was a living urban space which flowed in a dynamic manner, something totally unimaginable in modern Tokyo.

Referring to the construction of this city, beautiful as a 'garden', in which the groups of houses, the vegetation and the water were combined in an extraordinary fashion, Hidenobu Jinnai asserts that it 'can be interpreted as a balance between the "desire for planning", common to all cities that grow up around a castle, and the "flexible adaptation to the uneven terrain" of the Musashino highlands':

A clear and strong urban structure that would dominate the surrounding space was not created. Rather the area was carefully studied, taking the terrain with its delicate changes of level as a reference, and a pattern traced that was similar to a harmonious mosaic embedded in the ground, with the aforementioned individual urban elements distributed in an appropriate manner.[1]

So it appears that the garden-city called Edo consisted of an area in which the artificial elements, such as buildings, roads and canals, blended in with nature at all levels, forming a single space. In other words, it seems to me that technology and nature were fused into a single system, from the urbanistic macro-scale that formed the general plan of the city to the micro-scale that coordinated the relations between the individual houses and the gardens.

From the Meiji period onwards, new and artificial elements, such as means of transport, were introduced into this extraordinary space that destroyed the balance in a one-sided way. In particular, the increase in the size of the buildings and the introduction of the network of expressways, together with the rapid economic development of the postwar period, contributed in a decisive fashion to the elimination of the natural system.

In the Tokyo of today the confusion created by the tyranny of technology and the accumulation of hetero-geneous systems is evident. In my view, however, it makes more sense to try to discover the fascination of what is concealed in the urban space of our own day than to complain about the disastrous conditions of modern Tokyo and to look back with nostalgia to Edo, the garden-city of the past.

In comparison with the urban space of Edo, it is clear that Tokyo has lost the dynamic fluidity of plants and water. As I have already pointed out, what has increased instead is the flow of artificial elements. In the centre of the metropolis, in particular, vast systems of transport have been superimposed on one another at different levels, from a depth of tens of metres under the ground up toward the sky. At each level there is a highly complex horizontal transport network, linked to the other horizontal networks by a vertical system. In different zones of the metropolis these networks form different layers, something that could certainly not have been imagined in ancient Edo.

In addition, it is significant that it is not just people and vehicles that flow through the city. The flows of energy and information have increased explosively, to the point where it can be said that these invisible currents are dominating the urban space to an ever greater extent. We cannot mould this space of information into visible images inasmuch as it does not constitute a physical network and can only be observed through terminals. Given the increase in electronic flows and consequently in data, urban space can only be phenomenological. In other words, the real urban space made up of works of architecture is overlaid with another that stems from phenomena such as light, sounds, images, et cetera. This phenomenological city also comprises different areas, from the space created by light and images in a totally spontaneous manner to the abstract one formed by the web of signs of the so-called media. As a phenomenon the city is, after all, a space with a transient function (effect), generated by the invisible flow of electrons, and does not assume a morphological expression. The city-as-phenomenon transforms the real city into an illusory one, coated with light, sounds, images and signs. If we were to eliminate the concrete part, an enormous quantity of energy would be revealed, along with the network of electronic flows that manipulates this illusion.

As a consequence, the spatial characteristics of the contemporary city are fluidity, a multiplicity of layers and phenomenality, exactly the same as those of the microchip.

Nevertheless, I believe that describing this city as a 'garden of microchips' would be an excessive idealisation, on account of the overwhelming presence of the artificial objects introduced during the process of modernisation, of the networks of different means of transport that ignore the natural relief, of filled-in canals and above all of groups of huge buildings that completely ignore the natural flow. So we have to bring to light the delicate network of flows covered up by these other presences, as if we were carrying out an archaeological dig.

Could we not uncover the structure and the natural flow historically present within the constructions of the machine age, superimpose on them the networks of the electronic era and allow the whole thing to be recreated as phenomenological space? Only then would it be possible to describe this city as a 'garden of microchips'; only then would the superimposed layers of the networks of new technologies and the flow of nature itself begin to give rise to reciprocal effects.

ARCHITECTURE AS A DEVICE FOR STORING AND TRANSMITTING INFORMATION

If urban space today has already been transformed into a garden of microchips, is it possible to give this phenomenological space a concrete expression in the form of architecture?

I have always conceived my architecture by superimposing it on a garden, which means that I saw my works as gardens and not that my aim was necessarily to create an architecture that blended into the landscape. Nonetheless, in several of the projects I have produced in recent years I have tried to integrate the architecture into the landscape. So I have attempted to conceal the volume of the buildings or to establish a positive relationship between the individual buildings and the space outside by removing or adding earth. These intentions were very stimulating in themselves. In addition, the insertion of a natural environment of artificial form between buildings in the urban areas of Japan, where it is difficult to find a context between the constructions, seemed an effective stratagem.

Yet when I talk about architecture as a garden, I am thinking of an architecture as fluid and phenomenological as urban space. It does not reveal itself as a whole straightaway. Rather, it is people who link up the phenomenological spaces that succeed one another in each scene, in such a way that the overall image emerges in the end as a continuous series of all the scenes.

The scenes should not remain detached like the rooms of a building. What I want to create is a space in which some of them leave room for the following ones, leaving behind a sort of echo, just as happens in a film in which the images progressively appear and disappear.

It can be argued that architecture in which the temporal sequence takes on a fundamental importance is closer to the space of sound than to that of vision. It is a space in which innumerable sounds float. Of course these are not sounds emitted at random like those of urban space; rather they are selected in such a way as to insert them in a relationship based on choice. Not even the whole is organised into a form, like a classical music score or a Japanese *kaiyu* garden. As far as the choice of sounds to be combined is concerned, everyone can pick the ones that he or she prefers. As a consequence, even though there is a musical space that generates the score, the chronological order in which the notes are placed varies from person to person. For me, architecture understood as a garden has the image of a soundscape.

Yet my first attempt to produce a work like a garden, the House at Nakano or the White U, resulted in a space that resembled a *kaiyu* garden. A 'garden of light' was created between two concrete walls that curved to form a U. A luminous space rich in effects of light and shade, produced by the natural illumination from above and the sides, was formed within this tubular ring of spotless white. The phenomenon of light was used to create a space filled with currents and vortices. People entering the space could linger for a moment but could not change their route. They were only allowed to circulate around the empty space in the middle of the courtyard. The space was vigorous because the simplicity and clarity of the closed ring made it so, alluding precisely to a complete universe, ie to the force of cosmology, just like in a *kaiyu*.

The recently completed ITM Building in Matsuyama could also be described as a 'garden of light'. Rather than the White U's interior enclosed by concrete, what has been created here is a space filled with delicate light wrapped in translucent glass; the intensity of the light is controlled by a transparent membrane. The various architectural elements situated inside this volume of light reveal their dimensions in a horizontal as well as a vertical direction, maintaining a gradual relationship between them as if they were sounds wafting through the air. Although the horizontal and vertical relations are maintained, the terms 'above' and 'below' have little significance here. Hence those architectural elements whose significance derives from their relationship with the force of gravity, such as floors, walls and roofs, have been lost and even if we were to imagine the space rotated through 90 or 180 degrees, their significance would not change at all. The floors, stairs, partition walls, etc are made of translucent panels that let light through. Inside this new 'garden of light' the public, no longer confined by gravity, can walk around freely choosing sounds (the architectural elements) and singing their own musical notes.

If the House at Nakano and the ITM Building in Matsuyama are 'gardens of light', the Silver Hut and the Municipal Museum of Yatsushiro are 'gardens of wind'. What the two projects have in common are their continuous, light and thin vaulted roofs, constructed out of a framework of steel slats, and the free space between the independent columns that support them. Should not such a space be regarded as a garden that induces currents of air, like the wind blowing through a wood? In the case of Yatsushiro in particular, the different scenes staged vary in sequence: the curved bridge built on the top of a small hill covered with vegetation, followed by the space under the vaults that offers a view from an elevated position and then the exhibition hall with its supports resembling a natural clump of trees, the room open to the sky that offers a totally different space next to the entrance of the museum, etc. This building has been assigned the function of a museum, but a garden divided up into internal and external areas has been created in the zone that serves as the exhibition space proper. Visitors perceive the currents and vortices of air, and by walking and stopping weave the 'garden of the wind'.

My interest in electronic phenomena commenced with the Tower of Winds in 1986. The project cannot exactly be defined as a work of architecture, but it was the precursor of a series of works in which both light and images have been utilised. At the base of the Tower of Winds lay the intention of selecting the air (wind) and sound (noise) from the various currents flowing through the surroundings and turning them into luminous signs, ie into visual information. To put it briefly, it was a question of introducing information into the environment.

The project that I presented at the Yokohama 'Urbana Ring Exhibition' in 1992 had a similar aim. In this case, data on the conditions in Yokohama Bay had to be transformed into a visual and aural space by means of instruments like light, sound and images. The space of light and sound that resulted from this – and that was to have been called a 'media park' – was in reality another space of phenomenological water superimposed on that of the real water. Thus the project set out to turn information into environment and at the same time to introduce information into the environment itself.

So it might be asked how it is possible to transform data into environment in order to formalise architecture as a 'garden of microchips'. By its very nature the architectural act represents the creation of a new environment that is at one and the same time physical and phenomenological through the addition of information to the existing environment. In this case architecture becomes a device for emitting information and storing it. The architecture has no need of a physical form of its own but is transformed into a means of interpreting form as phenomenon (environment).

In the competition project for the University of Paris Library, drawn up last year, I also tried to create a work of architecture that could be used as a means of controlling the environment. In the first place, this consisted of a large oval room (centre) on a vacant site between three buildings of the university campus. That room is the information centre which, by linking the three constructions, transforms the free space from negative into positive.

In concrete terms, it is a functional space laid out around the reading room of the library, ie an instrument for the storage and transmission of information, since it is also a communication centre for students and teachers. The oval space is traversed by two levels of walkways arranged in parallel lines, architectural elements that make up the floor and ceiling and at the same time serve as a device for controlling the environment, for controlling light, sound and heat. They constitute a large horizontal slit for ventilation, making the oval room a pleasant place, suitable for reading. Just as these openings are devices for regulating the passage of light and wind, the two layers of walkways do not separate the interior from the exterior but create an environment that is similar to the outside, only more comfortable. So the concept of facade is absent from this architecture. However much the space is subdivided by panels of glass, you have the impression that it is continuous. On the one hand, what we have here is a device for the storage and transmission of information, a place in which the electronic flows form vortices; on the other we are in the presence of a mechanism for filtering light, heat (air) and sound, a place in which the flow of nature is modified. The oval and the line, respectively symbolising the two aspects, are superimposed, forming a layered space. So could not this project be considered the architectural realisation of the garden of microchips, inasmuch as it is characterised by fluidity, a multiplicity of layers and phenomenality, especially since such characteristics take the material form of architectural elements like walkways and screens?

The same concept of layered space has been adopted in the two projects still under construction in the municipality of Yatsushiro, the fire station and an old people's home. In both cases, what I wanted to create was a place that would not only be able to fulfil the functions specific to the two constructions but also resemble an open garden. In my view, in the first case it was not just a question of solving the problem of the physical construction of the layered space, but also of overlaying the specific functions of this fire-fighting park with the more ambiguous one of the garden and ensuring that these functions interacted with one another, creating a particular garden within the park as a consequence of their mutual permeability. The latter consists in the transparent relations between the two social functions, and is what we have to compose as materialised architecture. The situation is absolutely the same in the case of the old people's home.

Projects like the redevelopment plans for the city of Antwerp or the Luijazui central area of Shanghai also set out to create a 'garden of microchips'. Here it is easier to take real urban space as a reference, in so far as they are projects on an urban scale. By organising the multitude of networks present in the real urban space, and establishing a transparent relationship between the networks that form layers, new gardens appeal.

In any case I am convinced that the task of visualising the images of the microelectronic era coincides with the aim of designing the dream of the 'garden of microchips'. That is to say, it is a question of producing an electronic vortex in the space of the electronic current, of creating a place of information that will take the place of the *genius loci* of the past.

First published in *JA Library 2*, July 1993

NOTE

1. Hidenobu Jinnai, *Tokyo no kūkan jinruigaku* [*Tokyo: A Spatial Anthropology*] (Tokyo: Chikuma, 1985).

TARZANS IN THE MEDIA FOREST
(1997)

Mies's Barcelona Pavilion (1928–29) stands out as the most remarkable of all twentieth-century works of architecture. This is overwhelmingly true even in relation to all of the same architect's subsequent works. Nowhere else do we find a space filled with such 'fluidity'.

Although the structure is a combination of steel, glass and stone, it does not imply the hardness of these materials. The glass and stone are merely the flat and simple, planar components of the space. Spaces created by the combination of abstract, horizontal planes have an infinite extension, described by Sigfried Giedion as a mutual interpenetration of interior and exterior spaces. Similar effects can be found in works of that time by Frank Lloyd Wright and architects belonging to the De Stijl school, but none of them produces as strong a sense of fluidity as the pavilion in Barcelona. This is not simply because of its spatial composition, but owes a great deal to the brilliance of the materials. Everything, from the glass to the stone and metal, appears to fuse and flow out into the space. All the elements interact and create an atmosphere of eroticism within the space by their reverberation with the nearby surface of the water. The sensation created by the space is not the lightness of flowing air but the thickness of molten liquid. In the early 1920s, Mies made several drawings of skyscrapers. His later works, such as the Seagram Building and the Lake Shore Drive apartment houses, are generally considered to represent his idea of a high-rise. Personally, I think it is the pavilion in Barcelona that best embodies the image presented in those drawings. The space composed of glass is given no distinct structure but stands like a pillar made of ice, beginning to melt in the air. It is an architecture born out of images alone and does not yet have a definite form. Of course the pavilion in Barcelona has a structure and a form as it stands on the ground, but the original image of the glass architecture contemplated by Mies in his earliest days is brought vividly to life. This is a work of architecture in which the architectural style is not yet manifest.

Mies is said to be a proponent of the 'universal space' which swept through twentieth-century cities: a space created by a homogeneous continuum of grids extending both vertically and horizontally. True, Mies was one of the very first architects to come up with a skyscraper supported by a glass-and-steel curtain wall. And yet the image of a skyscraper that looks like a pillar of ice or the space embodied by the Barcelona Pavilion appear to differ considerably from the transparent office buildings that fill contemporary cities. The transparency of Mies's space seems to be entirely different from that of other modern architecture.

In the essay entitled 'Chicago Frame', Colin Rowe discusses this difference.[1] Rowe points out how the space defined by steel frames that already existed in late-nineteenth-century Chicago differs from the universal space studied by Mies van der Rohe. It is the difference between a space created as the result of a rational pursuit of pragmatic economic advantage and an ideological manifestation, symbolic of a future world based on technology. This difference, or antagonism, is still seen today between large corporate firms of architects and so-called avant-garde architects. Since there are no other architects who have been as faithful to the use of steel and glass as Mies, his buildings are unquestionably transparent. But the transparency of the Barcelona Pavilion is not that of clear air. Rather, it makes us feel as if we are looking at things deep underwater, and would better be described as translucent. The infinite fluidity we sense in the pavilion must arise from this translucent, liquid-like space. What we experience here is not the flow of air but the sense of wandering and drifting gently underwater. It is this sensation that makes the space distinct and unique.

The simultaneous fluidity and density of the
Barcelona Pavilion gradually disappeared even from
Mies's own architecture. Its place was soon taken by
architectural formalism instead. The once fluid space was
lost, as if a liquid had been turned into a solid. And as
we await the arrival of the twenty-first century, we are once
again in search of an erotic architecture that fuses with
the environment.

One night I was given the opportunity to speak at
the side of the pool next to Mies's now restored pavilion,
using visual images reflected in the water. Several days
later, I landed on Lanzarote in the Canaries. The island
was a staggering place. It was quite unlike anywhere else
I have ever been and far exceeded our expectations. It felt
like sitting on the sea bottom. The island must once have
been submerged by the sea. There was little fertile soil for
plants to grow and most of the surface was covered by
rock, gravel and sand. Strong winds must blow constantly,
as there were no plants that grew higher than the waist
of a human being. In spite of the fact that it was mid-sum-
mer, the plants looked withered and had hardly any green
leaves. The bare bushes resembled a coral reef – a coral
reef on dry land, the terrain of the sea bottom exposed
on the surface.

Underwater, organisms have far greater flexibility
than on dry land. On dry land, gravity makes it necessary
for fauna and flora alike to be armoured with a rigid and
self-supporting framework. Animals can never overcome
the rigidity of motion imposed by this framework. But
in water, the bodies of animals are subjected to pressure
as well as the effects of buoyancy. Pliant and flexible
structures stand up better to the flow or pressure of the
water. It is better to be receptive and surrender to the forces
than to resist them. Thus aquatic flora and fauna tend to
sway and dance gracefully. These motions define the forms
of living beings. The forms of aquatic creatures represent
motions more explicitly than those living on the land. The
forms of living beings are the loci of their motions. Indeed,
they are 'fluid bodies'.

What characterises the Sendai Mediatheque project is the tubular columns that support the floors in six tiers. The slabs, measuring about 50m on a side, are supported by 13 tubes that act as the structure. Each tube is made up of a combination of thin steel pipes and looks like a bamboo basket. The tube houses the means of vertical distribution, such as lifts and stairways, ducts for the air-conditioning system and conduits for the power supply, but it is essentially hollow. Natural light enters from the top of the tube. The tubes have different sizes and shapes depending on the functions they house. The design can be modified to adapt to the plan of the corresponding floor. In other words, these tubes are organic in nature, resembling plants in their forms and actions. They can be said to be biomorphic structures.

On the drawings that I made at the very first stage of the project I scribbled the words 'seaweed-like columns' next to the tubes. The columns were conceived as structures that sway and dance like seaweed in the water. Thus the volume, measuring 50m on a side and about 30m in height, is the embodiment of a tank of water. What we had pictured in our minds was 13 tubes softly swaying in the virtual water that fills the tank.

The Sendai Mediatheque is a new type of public facility that features a library and art galleries. Naturally, it should be a model library and a model museum of the next generation, equipped with an advanced computer network. What is the true image of an architectural space where new media are used in abundance? Why must we picture the space intended for electronic media as 'water' or as 'fluid bodies in water'? A graphic designer skilled in the use of the computer says he has the odd sensation that part of his body starts to flow into the screen whenever he sits at a computer. 'The inside of a computer is of course not inside myself, but it is not outside either.' The boundary is vague and he cannot tell how far the self extends. In the electronic media, time and space are different from those we experience in daily life. As we step into their world, as the designer says, 'a strangely comfortable sensation surges up inside me'. And he goes on, 'when I am sitting at a computer, I feel like I'm wading in the water's edge, that I am being linked with another world'.[2]

Fluids such as blood and lymph make up some 50 to 60 per cent of the human body and more than 80 per cent in the case of a newborn child. We may compare the human body to a stream insofar as fluids flow and circulate inside it. It connects with the world by means of water. Notwithstanding the fact that people, even today, cannot live without water, the system by which it is supplied to us is completely hidden from our eyes in contemporary cities. And we tend to forget that our bodies are part of nature. But we are reminded of this fact very clearly if we pay a visit to Bangkok. The city of Bangkok has a very well-developed network of canals and a large number of people live by and on the water. Looking at the way they live, we realise that our own lives must once have been very closely related to water. Water jugs stand in line on terraces. People dip and bathe in the turbid water and wash their clothes and dishes in the canal. They live like amphibians. Watching them, we can understand why Buckminster Fuller assumed that humankind originated at the waterfront in Southeast Asia.

The fact that the Thais worship Naga, the god of water, supports this. The gently rippling sea-snake Naga frequently adorns buildings and ships in Thailand. The elegant movements of Thai dancers also remind us of Naga. It is hard to believe they have the same rigid skeleton as other terrestrial organisms. Rather, they seem to lead a supple existence like plants and animals that sway and dance in the water.

The graphic designer poses a serious question when he says, 'just as water makes us realise that a human being is part of a greater nature, electronic media may modify or change the meaning or boundary of a human being, especially of the individual'. By entering into the computer screen, he became aware of the possibility of orienting the self toward the outside, a self that used to be excessively introverted. In other words, recognising the flow of

electronic media inside him made him realise once
again that the human body is part of nature. The new
technology is not antagonistic to nature. Rather, it is
creating a new kind of nature. If nature as we have always
known it is to be considered real, then this artificial nature
should probably be called virtual. And we people of
the modern age are provided with two types of body to
match these two types of nature: the real body which is
linked with the real world by the fluids flowing inside it,
and a virtual body linked with the world by the flow
of electrons.

In the East, 'nature' has always meant the basic
principle of the cosmos. In 4 BCE, for example, the Chinese
philosopher Lao-tzu taught that nature continues along
its own path in accordance with cosmic rules regardless
of any human act. According to this philosophy, the human
body is not independent of the world but an integral part
of a continuum that links it with the world.

Banzan Kumazama, a Japanese philosopher of the
early Edo period (seventeenth century), discussed the
integrity and continuity found in humankind and nature
in terms of the Neo-Confucian concept of *ki* or 'spirit':

**As our body is born from nature and nurtured by it, we
human beings exist in nature as its children, no matter
how small we may be physically. The *ki* of yin and yang and
the five elements that fill the heaven and the earth make
up our body. Turbid and thick *ki* takes a physical form and
becomes the body, while clear and light *ki* fills the inside
of the body to make it act.**

**Circulating in the cosmos like air, the spirit, or *ki*, becomes
condensed and solidified to form the bodies of organisms.
Bodies are made up of liquid and solid, but basically they
are gas. The gas condenses and solidifies to form the body,
and the air is taken inside and fills the body. Once inhaled,
the air is quickly exhaled again, and there is no distinction
between the self and others.**[3]

According to this way of thinking, each creature in the cosmos is given a certain form, but creatures are all fluid and constantly changing. They continually undergo phase shifts from gas to liquid to solid while remaining linked with the world. 'All things are in flux' indeed.

In the modern era, however, this cosmic view was forgotten, and people began to attach importance to the individual, physical body. People are now obsessed with a way of thinking that places the individual at the centre of the world, and then dissects the world into pieces. We have lost sight of human relations rooted in the community and are now beginning to lose sight of blood ties as well. Today, even the family unit is no longer secure. People end up as isolated beings and start to feel alienated and empty.

Just as we reached this point, electronic technology began to emerge and reminded us of the world we had almost forgotten. The 'flow of electrons' overlapped with the flows of *ki* and water.

Electronic devices such as personal computers, fax machines, mobile telephones and car navigation systems alter our physical senses from day to day. Mobile telephones are an essential tool for today's high-school students. They carry them wherever they go and are constantly communicating with their peers. For them, talking with their friends over the mobile telephone is like chewing gum. It is not their mouths but their eardrums that demand stimulation. By hearing the voices of their friends at all times, they seek to avoid being left alone. Their bodies crave the flow of electrons just as they need water and air.

A car navigation system also alters our physical senses. It allows us to confirm the position of our cars by radio waves transmitted from a satellite. The location of a car and the instructions needed for it to reach its destination are displayed on the screen at all times by means of a map on CD-Rom. With a conventional map printed on a sheet of paper, our physical bodies existed on a different plane, outside the map. The space on the map was abstract and we had to translate it into a three-dimensional space in our minds in order to learn the actual location by comparing it with reality. With the new system, the location of a car on the display overlaps with reality. We no longer have to dislocate our physical bodies to a different plane from that of the real world.

As the aforementioned graphic designer said, our isolated self is linked with the outside world by means of electronic media whether we like it or not. The concept of inside and outside is deeply rooted in the autonomy of the self. The emergence of new media obscures the boundary between the inside and the outside without our realising it.

When viewed from that angle, we have to admit that the real, physical body and the virtual one no longer contradict one another but overlap completely. To an analytical mind, there may appear to be a division into two bodies, but in fact they are integrated and unified. If we are determined to make a distinction, we could say that the former is an analogue kind of body which is not transparent, while the latter is a digital body and transparent.

What I have said so far about the physical body also applies to architecture and urban space. We have long defined architectural and urban space as something independent of nature. In Asia, however, they were extensions of nature and therefore fused with it. They maintained a relative position in nature and were alive, breathing in and out in response to the natural flux. The boundary between inside and outside was vague both in architecture and in urban spaces.

The houses that line Bangkok's canals clearly show us that the people who live there are totally free from the architectural concept of inside/outside. Broad terraces overhang the water, stairs run down into it and rooms are usually left open onto the terrace. Bougainvillea in full bloom almost invades the houses. Even though the canals provide their essential means of transport, their homes are left exposed to them, defenceless. There is no vanity or concealment. Here the concept of inside/outside refers to the relationship between architecture and environment and not to that of interior/exterior in the symbolic sense it has in society. An ideally comfortable relationship is formed between a human being and nature as there is no boundary between inside and outside, no matter how poor he or she may be. Not very long ago, we used to live like this in our traditional houses. People in contemporary cities, however, can no longer return to such a life even if they see it as a kind of utopia. It would be inconceivable for them to give up their mobile telephones or fax machines.

So what kind of environment should people be looking for when they are surrounded by electronic devices?

Marshall McLuhan once said that clothing is an extension of our skin and that shelter is the communal skin or clothing. As early as the 1960s he predicted that the development of electronic media would cause our then heavily vision-oriented culture to shift toward a dependence on cutaneous sensations. If we are to define hearing as one of the cutaneous senses, people fitted with electronic devices like a cyborg will no doubt grow obsessed with cutaneous sensations. Young people who cannot live without a mobile telephone need to stimulate their skin continually through their organs of hearing.

If, as McLuhan said, clothing and architecture are both extensions of our skin functioning as mechanisms for controlling energy and protecting us from the world outside, then their function as membranes would certainly be very important. In other words, clothing, architecture and cities must train and polish their epidermises (outer layers) to make them extremely sensitive and delicate. This epidermis can no longer be the conventional thick and heavy layer of cloth or wall that used to protect us from the outside world. It must operate as a highly efficient sensor capable of detecting the flow of electrons.

Moreover, the membrane needs to be soft and flexible. Rather than being rigid and dense like a wall, architecture as epidermis must be pliant and supple like our skin and be able to exchange information with the world outside.

It would be more appropriate to call architecture clad in such a membrane a media suit. Architecture is an extension of clothing and therefore a media suit. It is a transparent suit meant for a digitalised and transparent body. And people clad in transparent media suits will live in virtual nature, in the forest of media. They are Tarzans in the media forest.

First published in *2G*, 5 January 1997

NOTES

1. Published in *The Mathematics of the Ideal Villa and Other Essays* (Cambridge, MA: MIT Press, 1976).
2. *Asahi Shimbun*, 19 July 1994.
3. Toshio Kuwako, *Kisō no tetsugaku* [*Philosophy of Kisō*] (Tokyo: Shinyosha, 1996).

SHEDDING THE MODERN BODY IMAGE: IS A HOUSE WITHOUT CRITICALITY POSSIBLE?
(1998)

RIFTS WITH CONTEMPORARY SOCIETY

It is already 28 years since the completion of the first house I designed, and so my first message to society through the medium of architecture also dates from that time.

It seems certain that the status of architecture in the city is rapidly losing social significance. Yet if one continues to design as a lone, fragile person after the unparalleled futile collapse of the logic of the architectural world, the only available option is to expose the surrounding absurdities for what they are... For me, the design of a house is just the task of tracing the insurmountably deep rift between myself, as the designer, and the client, as the eventual inhabitant of the house. Rather than 'tracing', I should perhaps use the expression 'filling', but nowadays a shared terminology for filling the gap barely exists. As a consequence, the task can only begin with the contradictory acts of acknowledging the deep rift and building walls that cannot be backfilled.[1]

Hence for me the act of design begins with a personal expression of my unbearable frustration with regard to the state of society and the city. I openly expressed such sentiments with almost meaningless tubes of light protruding upwards, or aluminium-clad exterior walls that appeared rough and uneven when hit by sunlight. These were my only possible – and therefore strongest – acts of criticism at that time. Over the last ten years, I have been designing mostly public buildings. My feelings toward the design of public facilities are now almost the same as the message I cast into that small house of 28 years ago. A shared language able to fill the gap with real cities and social systems is virtually non-existent. We are merely stunned by recognition of these profound rifts. More than once, I have felt like flinging a model or walking out during a meeting with municipal authorities. But recently, what crosses my mind at such times is a fear that, faced with these rifts, I may have closed myself off from society. It is a fear that I may be using the comforts of critical speech to selfishly justify my own denial of reality.

It is not only in architecture that the manifestation of creative acts often emerges from a sense of anger or frustration toward the outside world. This is often the result of neurosis or irritation at not being able to directly express one's feelings. Whether hot or cool, such feelings are connected to a desire for personal expression. However, even though they somehow originate from individualistic impulses, these expressions will become detached from the hands of their creators, taking on an independent existence. Paintings or novels may be corralled within museums or bookshops, but architecture will suddenly alight in the sur-roundings. When it appears unmediated before a person's eyes, its effect is instant. Beyond this, it also serves people's daily lives, or is used for specific purposes. Architects have to confront the issue of the social or public nature of their expressions. The main problem I have encountered in designing public buildings over the past 10 years relates to whether it is possible to return to society a negative expression that repudiates society, as a direct individual expression of a negative or challenging form emerging from personal feelings of frustration and anger. Or, without losing the manifestation of energy, is it possible to replace negative impulses with a more positive expression of trust toward people?

However, from the moment an individual house is completed, it exists independently in a particular environment. Even private property is not necessarily precluded from being returned to society. If so, this seems to raise the same problems as public buildings. While this may be logically correct, with public buildings there is a difference in the actual design process.

THE MISUNDERSTANDINGS SURROUNDING CRITICISM

The moment I became involved with designing public facilities, opportunities to design houses seemed to disappear – which was not my intention. Two years ago, though, I was finally able to design two houses. In both cases, I was lucky with the clients and was inspired by how much I enjoyed designing houses. More than mere enjoyment, I felt a true pleasure in looking at houses.

Both houses had low budgets and because their sites were surprisingly large in volume most of the material finishes had to be cut back – they actually ended up being finished to the level of small workshops. The completion of the houses involved tense yet mild arguments with the clients. For the first time in many years, I held the conviction that it was possible to share a space with the clients. Because of this sense of sharing, the spaces, although extremely simple, did not descend into radical expressions.

Such a sense of sharing cannot be achieved in public buildings. In the development of any project there are momentary feelings of sharing a space with the specific people involved, yet on the whole, communication could be described as a series of gaps, ridden with rifts that are too difficult to fill.

I have used the word 'criticality' to denote the existence of such discontinuities. During one particular symposium I asserted, 'in the design of houses, there is no criticality'. That was my candid feeling immediately after completing those small houses. Expressing it seemed natural to me. I did not feel that there was a rift, or any need to directly express my anger and frustration. Being able to design while entirely detached from my usual insistence on the language of criticism, although somewhat bewildering, was also somehow pleasing. However, as I thought that this was probably a uniquely personal stance, I added the proviso, 'of course this also depends on the meaning of the word "criticism"…'

Consequently, I was very surprised to find that my statement about the absence of criticality in houses provoked comments along the lines of, 'is this guy intending to design only public buildings and no longer interested in pursuing the theme of house design?', or 'are established architects no longer looking at the design of houses?' I felt miserable at being so misunderstood, but I do not want to lower the discussion to this level.

It might be interesting to take the theme of house criticism and try to extrapolate my own personal feelings into a slightly more general theory. At the time I designed my first house in the 1970s, I thought that being critical of society was a virtue for an architect. However, this could probably be described as a notion present throughout the modern era. As modernist architecture was intended to transform society, it constantly assumed a negative posture toward existing social structures. Moreover, being rejected by society was always seen as a virtue. Yet until architects find more positive ways to engage with society, that is to say, until they abandon the word 'critical', it seems that they will continue to make exclusionary architecture. The house appears to be the easiest genre in which to take the first step toward escaping this narrow path.

Consequently, the thematic viewpoint here is not, 'is there criticality in a house?' but rather, 'is a house without criticality possible?'

A GROUP WITH A CLOSED AESTHETIC SENSIBILITY

While writing this text, I tried looking over the houses designed by young architects that have appeared in the magazine *Jūtaku Tokushū* over the last two years. I saw numerous shared symptoms. They have pure cubic shapes and tend toward transparency. Isamu Hasegawa, in his monthly column in the April 1998 issue of *Jūtaku Tokushū*, skilfully described what might be called the 'transparency syndrome' in this series of houses, and I will quote him here:

Structures framed with steel or wood, extremely large openings, an unusual concern with transparency, a few vertical walls that are white and flat, neutrality everywhere, and absolutely no pretence of structural strength... Overall, this series of houses gives an ephemeral, light impression, yet on the other hand each one looks like an undistinguished example of work from the 1920s avant-garde, the influence of which subtly infuses their shapes... these houses are being designed by young architects who were mostly born after 1960. Faced with this type of design, my sense of taste goes numb and I lose the ability to speak.

Although editorial selection may play a part, houses of this flavour are certainly conspicuous. Of course, many of these characteristics apply to my own architecture, and I am aware that due to my advocacy of lightness, ephemerality and transparency, I must bear some of the responsibility for this syndrome among my colleagues born only 20 years after me. Nevertheless, I have to sympathise with Hasegawa's loss of his faculties of speech and taste because, I suppose, I feel that many of these houses share a feeble introversion. Of course there are some exceptions, but most have a light and transparent aesthetic sophistication throughout. However beautiful and delicate, they do not engage with the exterior and are somehow negatively closed to reality. Put another way, while persisting with the modernist critique of society, I think an overwhelming number of these houses fail to clearly demonstrate any criticality of their own. I think that very few attempt to positively engage with reality.

But if one traced the roots of the negative criticism that can be seen in this group of houses, they would surely lead right to the 1920s. They obviously adhere to the language of modernism and a critical attitude toward reality that was a strong characteristic of early modernist architecture. As touched on earlier, I have also insisted that my own architecture be critical. Yet I cannot help thinking that a negative expression toward real society causes one to become detached from the land, and to turn one's back on the land.

A HOUSE OF PUREST MODERNISM, OR, THE TRAGEDY OF O'GORMAN

This spring, I curated an exhibition at a Tokyo gallery that featured a single house, constructed in the early 1930s. It was the recently restored residence of Diego Rivera and Frida Kahlo, a modernist house located in Mexico City. While visiting Mexico last year, I was lucky enough to have the opportunity to visit the house, although until then I had known absolutely nothing about it. I did not even know the name of its designer.

Yet the moment I got out of the car in front of the site, I was powerfully moved by the house. Firstly, it had a pure and stoic shape that totally overturned my preconceived images of Mexico. Designed by Juan O'Gorman for two intensely individualistic painters leading a tumultuous life, this house was completed in 1932. It is almost contemporaneous with Le Corbusier's Villa Savoye, completed in 1931.

The two painters were married but worked independently, so two separate buildings were provided, each containing a residential space and an atelier. Linked only by a bridge hanging from the rooftop, the two buildings are simple, clear, cubic shapes that seem to be floating. Painted Indian red and marine blue respectively, strongly evocative of Mexico's natural environment, the two volumes are surrounded by a cacti hedge and supported by *pilotis* that disengage them from the ground. Using the language of pure modernism, the architecture is not only separated from the earth, but also appears completely independent of the Mexican land, which is still infused with a sense of regionalism.

When discussing contemporary Mexican architecture, what immediately comes to mind is the work of Luis Barragán, which has a completely different character to the house by O'Gorman. Barragán's houses blend far more softly with the Mexican climate. Compared to O'Gorman, their vivid colours only intensify the harmony with the Mexican natural environment, and their coarsely textured surface finishes or the use of timber in the deep openings only heighten the intimacy of their relationship with the land. While their overall volumes are based on the language of modernism, this is not conspicuous but is softened and entwined with vegetation to minimise confrontation with the environment. In other words, I feel that the architecture of Barragán is a modernism that yields to the land in a revisionist truce with the region. It offers a way of life that may not be particularly new, but is rich, calm, and stable.

On the other hand, O'Gorman's Rivera–Kahlo House vibrates with suggestions for a new, modern way of life. When he designed this house, O'Gorman was just 26 years old. The architect had only recently graduated and had never even visited Europe. I do not understand how he could accomplish a house of such a high standard, but I am certain that he was strongly influenced by Le Corbusier's work and ideas.

It is clear that Rivera's wing in particular, with its serrated roof and open-air concrete stair, took conceptual hints from the Ozenfant Atelier (1923), but looked at in terms of functionality, it is even more resolved than Le Corbusier's early houses. The pursuit of rationality and economy was taken to the extreme in elements such as the stairs, walls, floors and columns, right up to the structural calculations. The same goes for the delicacy of the plans and elevations, and every detail of each element (doors, window frames, dust shoots, drainpipes, furniture) was attained by thinking purely in terms of functionality and economy.

O'Gorman's attempt at pure functionality can be clarified by a comparison with Le Corbusier's early master-pieces, the Villa in Garches (1927) and the Villa Savoye (1931). Like the Rivera–Kahlo House, these houses are based on clear-edged, simple geometric volumes, but their inherent architectural meanings are different. While saying that they were proposals for a new way of life and were in pursuit of function, Le Corbusier's houses skilfully incor-porated classical architecture on the one hand, and abstract painting on the other. As Colin Rowe has pointed out, their exteriors can be superimposed with the articulations and proportions of a Palladian villa, and their interiors are an accumulation of layers similar to the curves used in purist paintings.[2] In other words, while Le Corbusier continued to advocate new proposals for new cities, he simultaneously incorporated the systems of historical architecture and the experimental methods of avant-garde artistic movements.

Seen in this light, Le Corbusier's *Five Points for a New Architecture* (1926), which was intended to enable a new way of life, seems to be only a means of justifying his own architecture using the logic of modernism. Rather than Le Corbusier, it was the 26-year-old O'Gorman who really made a pure depiction of the dream of a new way of life based on the five principles of *pilotis*, roof gardens, horizontal strip windows, the free plan and the free facade. In the Rivera–Kahlo House, these five proposals are indeed implemented purely as social proposals. Perhaps it is only in this moment of the earnest pursuit of function that the language of modernism burst from its closed context and sublimated its character as a critical language. This is evinced by the pride taken in this exclusively modernist space by Rivera and Kahlo, despite their fanatical promotion of the bloodlines of ancient Mexico and their support for the communist movement.

However, O'Gorman did not continue his search. In the first half of the 1930s, he was involved with many social programmes, such as schools and mass housing, but from the mid-1930s on he abandoned architecture and took up painting. Influenced by Rivera, he later threw himself into the mural movement. Although maintaining his commitment to social reform, he turned in a direction completely opposite to the pure, abstract spaces of Western European modernism. O'Gorman's conversion did not end there. In 1953, he started to live in a house he had built that looked like a cave filled with Amerindian ornaments. In 1982, he moved into a modernist house he had designed when young, and there he took his own life.

Perhaps as a result of launching himself into the pursuit of excessively pure and absolute modernist space, O'Gorman came to clearly see the rift between the land of Mexico and the language of modernism. This was undoubtedly an irreparable rift.

SHEDDING THE MODERN BODY IMAGE

The two worlds that Juan O'Gorman symbolically depicted during the course of his single life represent the two extremes of his own body image. These are the body as a concept, and the living body. The former is an unnatural body that aims at a consciously conceived abstract, utopian world; the latter is a natural body that extends to the traditions of ancient Mexico. People of every era constantly try to fix within their dwelling spaces those memories of the land that are etched into their flesh. These are not merely personal memories, but a spatialisation of the memories of a family or regional group. Houses that are built up in such a way, across generations of struggle with the violence of the natural world, become like a skin that extends the physical bodies of the people.

Yet at the same time, people have also continued to develop another kind of house, as a memory of the future. Amid the rapid development achieved this century, particularly in technology, people have been dreaming of various alternative houses. These are experiments in transposing the exhilarating sensation of being in automobiles or aircraft, in other words, the spaces of machines, into dwelling spaces. When their body is put inside a skin of steel, glass, aluminium or plastic, people relish the sense of bodily liberation, as if moving into another dimension. They then attempt to expand this sense of liberation into another skin, into another body. This is a liberation from the enchantment of the land, as well as a liberation from the customary way of life that links regional societies or families to the land.

I have referred to a body that seeks a house for future memories as an unnatural body, but this is now transforming into a body that may personally experience the universe. It is also possible to redefine this as a body that is seeking a new, different nature. In other words, having already expanded into a body seeking machines, it may begin to seek nature as a future memory. Accordingly, we may call such a body the 'virtual body'.

O'Gorman's Rivera–Kahlo House was a house sought by a body as a consciousness captivated by the era of machines. However, it failed due to a rejection of the body as a strong collective memory of the land. Restored to himself, he tried to entrust his own body to the memories of the land, and failed yet again. For him, the coexistence of these two bodies was unendurable.

Yet these two bodies still coexist in those of us living in modern times, and even the chaos of today's urban spaces can be regarded as the result of aiming at these two bodies. It seems that the current condition includes many architects who still see themselves as heirs to modernism and try to discuss architecture in that language, standing ambivalently without ever finding a place to set down. However, the power of the land that we encounter has been weakened by the processes of modernisation, and the body is exposed in an atrophied world of regionalism. There is no need to make a comparison with Mexico, which was undergoing a revolution at the beginning of the century, but it appears symbolic that, having passed the peak of modernisation, this group of architects has lost sight of the present condition of Japan. Hasegawa's loss of the ability to speak and taste was undoubtedly the result of his succumbing to these ambiguous shapes that lack the confidence to be heirs to modernism, and lack the power to meaningfully address society. To lose one's social language and become enclosed in a sophisticated aesthetic sensibility seems to be nothing more than using the negative language of criticism to justify a pent up frustration. Perhaps this frustrated group of architects, as successors of modernism, must shed their bodies before they do anything else, because they have reached a deadlock in the confrontation between the two types of body wherein no more future memories can be produced. We must therefore consider depicting a new body image that sheds this confrontation. This is not an unnatural body, but is another body that is intimate with nature, and a body that also accepts our prior nature. When these two natures are superimposed, we might then begin to talk in a positive language about the kind of house sought by new bodies.

Originally published in *Contemporary Japanese Houses 1985–2005* (Tokyo: Toto Shuppan, 2005)

NOTES

1. From 'The Act of Designing is Just the Task of Tracing One's Own Distorted Thought Processes', *Shinkenchiku*, October 1971.
2. See Colin Rowe, *The Mathematics of the Ideal Villa and Other Essays* (Cambridge, MA: MIT Press, 1982) and Colin Rowe and Robert Slutzky, 'Transparency: Literal and Phenomenal', *Perspecta*, 8 (1963), 45–54.

THE SENDAI MEDIATHEQUE
AS A NEW DOM-INO SYSTEM
(1999)

Even though more than four years have passed since Sendai
City held the open design competition (in early 1995) the
Sendai Mediatheque is a work of architecture that is still
under construction. The completion of the building will
take another one and a half years, and it will be about two
years before it opens.

The Sendai Mediatheque is a mixed-use facility
centred on a local library and citizens' gallery. The competition design brief defined a 'mediatheque' as something
that 'supports each citizen as a creative individual, together
with the comprehensive accumulation and supply of art
images as emotional media, a library and various forms of
information as intellectual media, and their fusion as new
media, as well as providing images of spaces for new urban
functions in a new era.'

In a report from the Project Advisory Committee,
established after the beginning of basic design, it was
redefined as a facility that 'as well as being an accumulated
body of wisdom comprising contemporary information
technology as its infrastructure, can be used to generate
new symbols. Accordingly, what are conventionally called
libraries and museums are absorbed into a new system
that allows the active access of every citizen.'

The Sendai Mediatheque is therefore an attempt
to seek an image for a future library and museum
predicated on information networks. With this definition
as the basis, an information system advisory committee
proceeded to consider the present situation and the kinds
of information service that can be provided. The salient

themes in this discussion were the following
three points:

> 1. Rather than the conventional model of fixed,
> unidirectional services, it will be supported by the
> activities of user participation and self-expression.
>
> 2. Rather than a model of autonomous service within
> the building, it will aim at a shared service network.
>
> 3. The activity programmes will be constantly
> examined and new results incorporated, aiming at
> a self-generating facility.

Such discussions might seem unrelated to architectural
space, but the method of spatial composition may be considered to exert a large influence on the use of the building.

The spatial composition that we proposed in the
design competition is a system that could be called a 'New
Dom-ino'. That is to say, seven flat floors (50m x 50m steel
honeycomb slabs) are supported by 13 tubular structures
with absolutely no structural walls or braces. As well as
being used for duct spaces, pipe spaces and vertical
circulation, the interiors of the tubular structures convey
natural light from above into the interior, performing the
function of a decentralised core. Leaving aside the
differences in floor heights, the spaces of each floor
contained between two slabs, along with these larger and
smaller 13 tubes, are homogeneous from top to bottom.

The space of the 'New Dom-ino' system has been
devised to embody a composite informational space called
a 'Mediatheque' by means of the following spatial
characteristics.

ELIMINATING SPATIAL HIERARCHY

Whether libraries or museums, current public facilities are
the continuation, in some form, of spatial typologies that

have existed since the nineteenth century. Centrality and autonomy are strongly expressed, and the desire to create a microcosm cannot be abandoned. This kind of spatial hierarchy (static order) also fixes the activities taking place, and it is extremely difficult to escape from conventional, unidirectional, autonomous services.

In the 'New Dom-ino' system, homogeneous space is implemented all the way from layer one to layer seven. Any arrangements that would produce spatial hierarchies such as centrality and frontality are omitted. However, rather than a repetition of ubiquitous monotonous spaces, as in multi-storey office buildings, the composition gives rise to a lively sense of locality by means of changes in floor height, changes in light and the random layout of the tubes.

MAXIMUM ELIMINATION OF THE DISTINCTION BETWEEN INTERIOR AND EXTERIOR SPACES

The functionalism of modernist architecture clarified the boundaries between served areas (users' spaces) and service areas (managers' spaces) as a result of clearly separating the circulation routes of users and managers. Though such a division of circulation routes is necessary to some degree, in the planning of the Sendai Mediatheque the aim is to integrate service and served spaces. This is because I think it is essential to remove the barriers between the two in order to enable an interactive service model.

MAKING OPEN, EXTENSIVE SPACES

Public facilities that overemphasise the principle of efficiency tend toward a proliferation of small, insular rooms. They tend toward single spaces corresponding to single functions, with absolutely no consideration given to the relationships between them. However, human activities – in situations such as drinking coffee and reading while listening to music – are essentially integrated and diverse.

As a way of freely stimulating cultural activities through user participation and self-expression, insular single-function spaces are extremely inappropriate, and would be regressive for architecture in an era of information networks. Margins should be provided as creative spaces that can respond to flexible change. As many walls as possible should be removed.

These spatial characteristics have enabled the Sendai Mediatheque to interact with information networks, and even now various discussions are ongoing. Intense, and occasionally abusive, communication continues through emails between the people involved, such as the municipality, the members of the advisory committee and the designers. For a conventional public facility, this condition of debating the basic concept and plan while erecting the building as hardware would be an unthinkably strange situation.

However, this fact alone indicates that this architecture has already taken a step toward the implementation of user participation and interactive service. Rather than postulating a theoretical idealised image, in the Sendai Mediatheque there is the visceral feeling of a search for an as yet unknown public space undertaken within everyday reality.

ICHIRO-LIKE ARCHITECTS:
ON THE REALITY OF ARCHITECTURE
(2002)

A YOUNG GENERATION THAT DOES NOT ENGAGE IN DIALOGUE

Recently, I have come to feel that 'architecture has no reality' for young people aspiring to become architects. As people living in contemporary society, they do not seem to think about the meaning of architecture as it exists within that society.

In every era, young architects and students have rebelled against the preceding generation, framing their architectural theories in terms of their own feelings of being oppressed. Their impudent recklessness is a manifestation of surplus energy, a forgivable symptom of their youthful innocence and zeal. We expect that they will reinvigorate the architectural world. We expect that they will construct their architectural theories while converting their frustrations – resentment because they have no work, jealousy because their colleagues do – into personal energy. Occasionally, it is the seeming egotism of uncontrollable emotions of anger, resentment and jealousy that produces the most authentic personal realities. Thinking about an appropriate outlet for these emotions within society may be arrogant, but this is the soil from which vibrant architectural theories will grow.

Teaching at universities myself, and welcoming young people into my office, I have always embraced the potential of vivid ideas from young people, however conceited they may be. In designing architecture it is necessary to be experienced in the techniques for its implementation, but

experience is unnecessary at the brainstorming stage.
A lack of knowledge about the architectural world can
improve the chances of producing fresher, stronger images.

But recently, at universities as well as in my office,
it has become impossible to establish a dialogue with young
people. When provided with computers, many of them can
create splendid drawings. If asked to draw highly transparent and abstract architecture, they will create plenty of beautiful graphics. But when asked about the reasons for abstraction or transparency, they give no reply. Even when asked
about scale or proportion, they are mostly unresponsive.
They just sit in silence, intently facing their computer screen.
Discussions and debates do not provoke their interest.

There is certainly a change underway, which perhaps
could be encapsulated by the phrase 'corporeal transformation'. Previously, I have talked about the contemporary
body as the integration of two bodies, the real body and
the virtual body. I pursued the possibility of new spatial
images through the extensions of the virtual body enabled
by electronic technology. Only video-gamers, able to cast
their bodies into three-dimensional game-space, may
be entrusted with opening up dreams of new architectural
images in weightless, four-dimensional spaces. But however they may pioneer a body able to leap about on the
other side of the screen, no architecture can erase the
awareness of another, unchangeable body on this side of
the screen. It is still impossible for architecture to erase
the reality of the wheezing, aching, irritable body. There is
a feeling of emptiness brought on by my daily interactions
with young people – maybe it is because of my age, or
maybe it is because the architectural space of this emptiness, which is inaccessible to me, does not really exist.

UNCREATIVE JAPAN

However, the emptiness that I feel when confronted with
young people never subsides, because it is related to the
emptiness that I feel when confronted with the design of

public buildings in Japan. In other words, this emptiness seems to originate in the lack of creative spirit that now permeates the whole of Japanese society.

When engaged in the design of public facilities, I have no idea why I am making architecture or for whom I am making it. I forget the most primitive questions about the act of making architecture. I am only aware of constraints: don't do this, don't do that. In contemporary Japan, we seem to completely ignore the naïve question 'Why make architecture?'

Compared to any other country in the world, public facilities in Japan are built with a high degree of precision. 'Precision' as used here is not a question of precision in construction. Perhaps I should call it fastidiousness, which includes efficiency. Whether safety, whether heat and sound insulation, or efficiency of air-conditioning and lighting, every point is given exceedingly scrupulous consideration. Put conversely, design is nothing but the act of clearing an endless checklist of items. Their eyes bloodshot and their bodies exhausted, both designers and builders just keep on ticking boxes without proposing any ideas.

However, when these exhausted bodies are asked the purpose of the architecture they have finally completed, everyone is at a loss for words. At best, the answer is 'for the citizens'. Yet where might we stumble upon these abstract 'citizens'? Naturally, citizens are nothing more than discrete wholes possessing a range of independent feelings.

Japan today looks like a struggling corporation in a recession. It may produce flawless systems with staggering administrative capabilities and safeguards, but it lacks the joy of making. The entire organisation comprises highly integrated monitoring systems, but everyone stuck in this system collapses into autism.

Whether in architecture, cars or music, one expects the act of 'making' to contain a joy that fulfils the simplest human curiosity. In this complex society, one might be laughed at for saying such a thing, but perhaps what these strictly controlled Japanese companies most need is to pursue a simple 'joy of making'.

Japanese society is inundated with debates over whether to make or not to make. No matter how many conventional public facilities are built in Japan, they are mostly meaningless if their architecture does not pulse with individuality. A society that does not make anything has no option but to earnestly proceed down the road toward autism.

ARCHITECTURAL EXPERIENCE IN EUROPE

I have been involved in the design of temporary pavilions for two European cities, Bruges and London. The Bruges pavilion was built in the city centre, in the middle of the town hall square, as a monument commemorating the city's selection as the European Capital of Culture. It opened in February 2002, and was intended to be there for one year. For London, I built a summer pavilion on a beautiful lawn belonging to a contemporary art gallery in Hyde Park. This lasted for a mere three months.

Both cities are so full of architectural structures carved by history that they are like architectural museums. It is not easy to build new architecture in the centre of such cities, even if it's temporary. And although the two pavilions were described as temporary, their circumstances differed.

In the case of the Serpentine Pavilion in London – planned as an installation like an outdoor sculpture – I intended from the outset to create a contemporary expression. Daniel Libeskind and Zaha Hadid had already designed summer pavilions as part of the same pro- gramme, and the people of metropolitan London are highly appreciative of contemporary art. In other words, there was a strong predisposition to respond to its artistic qualities. But conversely, I had to be prepared for some harsh criticism if these qualities were deemed inadequate.

I was quite astonished by the energy expended on designing a pavilion that would last a mere three months and cost almost 100 million yen. Most of this money came from sponsors such as glass manufacturers and steel fabricators. Without admiration and praise for the sponsorship, a project like this would be impossible. In this context, I could understand the importance of attracting public interest.

Mass media such as newspapers, television and radio played an important role in raising the public's awareness of the project. Even before construction started, information was conveyed to the public, and more sponsors decided to participate after the level of interest became clear. The project started before the funding goals had been reached, and continued in a highly volatile state. The design process was subject to constant change, under conditions that did not allow us to predict whether or not the pavilion would be built. If we had insisted on building something with a minimal clarity of intention, the project could have evaporated in a fraction of a second.

In Bruges, the circumstances were identical. Initially, I expected a great deal of resistance, because instead of being built in a public park as in London, a pavilion with an aluminium structure was to be planted in the centre of a touristic city with a beautifully preserved medieval townscape. However, from the mayor on down, the majority of the citizens and mass media actively supported our proposal. What impressed me above all was their sincere enjoyment of the construction process.

During construction, pedestrians would pause, examine the daily changes in appearance, chat with us on the site, and without fail make some comments before they left. I felt that this small architectural act was located within the sphere of their everyday lives.

After both pavilions had opened – and, needless to say, on their scheduled opening days – many people visited: they were truly relaxed, walking dogs or pushing baby strollers.

In Bruges, there was almost no function, but in London the pavilion was used as a café, so many people sat around the tables every day and engaged in animated discussions about architecture. Occasionally it became a lecture space in which hundreds of people would gather, sitting or standing as they liked. In any case, the architecture was perceived in a truly natural way, and time spent there was fully enjoyed.

There is a certain dialogue about architecture that encompasses the users (citizens), the clients and the mass media, as well as the architects. With permanent structures, these relationships are even stronger.

In the case of a hospice that I am designing for the city of Paris, I finally received the building permit a short while ago, some two and a half years after the competition. It will be another six months at least before construction starts. The whole process is taking an abnormally long time, calling for intense endurance. The first year and a half following the competition was entirely taken up with arguing with the clients. Whether for the plans or the facades, detailed discussions were necessary. Particularly with regard to the facades, I went to Paris every month for half a year bearing new proposals, and had repeated arguments with the owners. It was not at all the case that they didn't like the proposals, but beyond getting approval for a highly transparent glass facade, the time-consuming arguments served the purpose of ensuring that our intentions were sufficiently understood and accepted.

A briefing for the local residents was then held. About 50 people gathered, and there was some incredibly vehement arguing back and forth. Strong voices of opposition were raised against the glass facade, but the clients unwaveringly defended our proposal.

Following this, the arguments spread beyond the construction site to the newspapers. While there are historians who have developed preservation theories for the evaluation of existing buildings that are more than 100 years old, critics also supported our proposal from the standpoint of revitalising the city.

The granting of a building permit depends not only on legal issues, but on whether or not the municipality feels that all arguments have been sufficiently heard. In any case, an enormous amount of time, energy and perseverance was required. However, this was only to be expected, given the significance of new architecture appearing in a city lined with historical architecture. In the drive to preserve European townscapes, this degree of argument and time is probably quite natural. Europe is not immune to the logics of selfishness, egoism and politics that frustrate architecture: there is no practice of rewarding good and punishing evil. But there is an unavoidable comparison to be made with the interminable repetition of dialogues and debates over the question 'What is the purpose of making architecture?' I cannot think about architecture as a cultural act without an intense envy of its location within society.

ACES IN AN ERA OF COOLNESS

Let us return to Japan, which is permeated by emptiness and bereft of purpose. Will the day come when architecture as culture takes root in the daily life of this country? What kind of architectural theories can emerge from the ambitions of those students and wannabe architects who have abandoned reality? Unlike the theories of our generation, which arose from an angry, resentful, envious, vital corporeality, perhaps a cooler, smarter architectural logic might be possible.

Among the wannabe architects who stare silently at their computer monitors all day long, there are a few young architects who have already gone into practice for themselves. These are people around 30 years old.

To be sure, they are trying to formulate their own methods with standpoints that differ from our generation. They have a smart, rational methodology that might be called 'cool-ism'.

In two recent competitions for which I was a jury member, I encountered a number of works that left a lasting impression. In essence, all of them seem linked in some way to the following three terms:

1. Patternism
2. New Abstractionism
3. Weak Realism

The international design competition for the new Tomihiro Art Museum, organised by Azuma, a village with a population of less than 4,000 located in the mountainous region of Gunma prefecture, attracted no less than 1,211 submissions from 54 countries. This might be considered a remarkable achievement in the architectural world of empty Japan, but what I found deeply interesting during the judging was the clear difference between the submissions from other countries and those from Japan. Generally speaking, the work from abroad was powerful and robust, while the work from Japan was sophisticated, delicate and abstract.

It is mysterious that the submissions from the foreigners, who we can assume did not see the site, were more real than the abstract submissions from the Japanese, who we can assume did see it. The impression of cool, smart, young Japanese architects was also clearly in evidence.

Among the submissions from Japan, three projects stood out. These were by Makoto Yokomizo, who was selected as the winner, Mitsuhiko Sato, who received an honourable mention, and Ryue Nishizawa, who made it to the final round of 18 proposals.

Yokomizo's proposal, since realised, was a 56m-square, 3.3m-high flat cube, characterised by a plan articulated only by means of larger and smaller circles. The exhibition rooms, the storerooms, the hall and the lobby all had circular plans, and along the periphery these circles were truncated by the lines of the exterior wall. Adjacent circles were independently circumscribed, connected only by apertures at the places where they touch. The leftover triangular spaces produced by the meeting of three circles became light gardens.

The novelty of this proposal lies in the complete lack of differentiation between purposive spaces and connective spaces. There is absolutely no spatial hierarchy. The design method is to first define the multiple rooms demanded by the competition brief as circles with the required floor areas, then arrange them like a puzzle while taking into account the strengths of their mutual relationships, and finally truncate them with a square frame. Perhaps a method in which the programme is handled by an assemblage of only the most primitive shapes – circles and squares – could be called patternism. In any case, the clarity and objectivity provided an impression of freshness absent from conventional methods. It had a coolness that seemed automatically programmed by a computer without the intervention of a designer.

Mitsuhiko Sato's proposal used a square plan of almost the same size. This proposal is characterised by a storeroom placed as a nested box in the centre, resulting in a peripheral space into which one folded line is inserted. The full extent of this folded line is the length of the required exhibition wall surface – the most important aspect of the programme for a museum. The new interior/exterior spaces demarcated by this line are also boundaries that divide the exhibition room/lobby, library and hall.

By focusing on the length of the exhibition wall surface as a folded line embedded in a square plan, this proposal also gave the impression of a plan that had been created automatically.

What these two proposals have in common is the skilful concealment of the designer's living body. However smart the resolution of the preliminary situation (hypothesis), in these processes the act of design appears to emphasise the lack of leeway for including the sentiments of an emotional individual. The process of transition from programme to space is abstract throughout, and very different from an interactive method. They show no notable interest in debating the programme itself. Their overriding interest is in the solution. Against that background, the programme is merely one hypothesis, and another hypothesis would have another answer. That is to say, to relativise the given conditions of a complex society and indicate an excellent solution is regarded by these architects as an expression of contemporary values.

Compared to the proposals of Yokomizo and Sato, I felt that Nishizawa's proposal for Gunma adhered more to expression than to method. In his proposal the white, abstract cubes of the exhibition rooms are just set at random orientations while being connected. Not following specific rules, the layout is more arbitrary than in the other two proposals, accentuating the abstraction of the cubes. The appearance of obsessively minimalist cubes arrayed without mediation amid nature had a degree of abstraction that stood out from the other competition entries. From the latter half of the 1960s into the 1970s, Kazuo Shinohara published a series of houses filled with white abstraction, and we were enthralled by the cold, inhuman spaces. Looking back on them now, however, those abstract backgrounds seem to teem with a stifled hot significance. Like the bare backdrops to Godard's movies of the time, they seem to speak volumes about their era. By contrast, the only message to be extracted from the abstraction contained in Nishizawa's expression relates to the obsessive deployment of white cubes. As an unprecedented type of abstraction, perhaps this could be called a new abstractionism.

In the competition for the Aomori Prefectural Museum of Art, which was held about one year prior to Gunma, the proposal from Sou Fujimoto – which competed with the winner Jun Aoki until the end, but regrettably finished as runner-up – had a markedly different appearance to the three works mentioned above. Decidedly unabstract, this proposal adopted a realistic expression. As if hidden among the trees, it is a truly calm and restrained composition comprising a series of finely articulated volumes with monopitch or gabled roofs. There was no reason to be provocative with regard to the programme, and a life-sized expression is shown at life-size. It is a work remarkable only for its gentleness, which is one characteristic of young people today. However, when he appeared alone for the competition interview, and nonchalantly began to say, 'I want to make weak architecture', the judges were rendered speechless. Compared to the other architects, who all attended the interviews accompanied by their engineers or staff members, his aloof appearance made an extremely strong impression on me. The provocation of a gentle work lies precisely in the theme 'weak architecture'. How can 'weakness' become a theme? To that question the Italian architect Andrea Branzi gives this answer:

It seems that we have entered an era of 'weak modernity'. This refers to weak energy like that characterised by electrons, weak technology like electronics, weak science like genetics, or contemporary thought that explains weak ideas, but I think that this might stimulate revolution at a deeper level... The word 'weak' does not have a negative meaning, but is a word that expresses the possibility of substantial change and a way of possessing a new consciousness. One could also say that a new ground plane is being opened...[1]

While greatly differing in expression from Yokomizo, Sato and Nishizawa, it appears that Fujimoto, in his debates and discussions with others, also does not think about the production of expression. I can only imagine that this amiable architect struggles alone with a calm expression on his face.

ICHIRO-LIKE ARCHITECTS

These four young architects can all be called children of the computer era. Whether abstract or real, perhaps their methods can cut through empty Japan as pioneering models for the introverted, speechless generation. Their methods somehow recall Ichiro's batting technique.

I once wrote, 'Ichiro bats as if he is playing a computer game.' This was at a time when he was still playing in Japan. Since then, no matter which pitcher he faces, Ichiro swings the bat as if responding to a pitching machine, completely calm, completely expressionless. Faced with any ball, he responds with cool, astonishing reflexes, and receives the ball perfectly. I described this manner as follows:

At that moment, Ichiro is not facing the pitcher of the opposing team, but is drawn into the space of the ball thrown by his opponent. This can be easily understood if one imagines the appearance of children absorbed in the spaces of video games. Whether Ichiro or a child immersed in a video game, they are not simply facing the ball or the screen through the sense of sight. They have entered a virtual space that engages all of their senses: hearing, touch, and so on.[2]

Six years have passed since I wrote that essay, but even now that he is in the major league, his appearance is completely unchanged – on the contrary, he continues to hone his technique of being drawn into the space of the ball. Among the brawny major-leaguers, the technique of the slender Ichiro seems delicate and sophisticated. He has truly mastered weak technology.

Then might the aforementioned four architects become the Ichiros of the architectural world? And might those young people who continue to lack a sense of reality be called Ichiro wannabes?

However, Ichiro is sustained by his unexpressed real body. I may say that he hits the ball as if playing a computer game, but at the final moment his opponent must propel a ball toward him at a speed of 150km/h. A living sensation is always transmitted to his hands through the bat. His body must store the strength to return the frighteningly animate ball to his opponent. This itself is nothing other than the reality of the body.

It is indeed the contemporary style to acquire a smart, cool method for using a computer. However, to implement this as architecture in society, the other, real body is absolutely necessary. Occasionally it may be necessary to expose one's vulgar body to public view and debate. Whether or not cool objectivism or weak realism can cut through to the next generation will depend on whether or not another, stronger body can be trained.

I would like to emphasise above all that architecture is a game lacking clear rules. Whether baseball or a computer game, one plays in accordance with rules. When the rules are removed, the game itself cannot exist. I am not saying that there are no rules in architecture, but that the frame is not clearly determined. Moreover, the most meaningful creativity in architecture might incorporate and expand upon changes in the rules of social frameworks. The absence or presence of reality in architecture depends on whether or not these social frameworks are recognised. The grounds for questioning reality are precisely here. The image of the 'architect' that exists within me is a dispute between the Europeans truly enjoying architecture in nature and the computer game experts, and at present I cannot get them to intersect.

NOTES

1. Andrea Branzi, quoted in *Shinkenchiku*, September 2001.
2. *Shitsunai*, March 1996.

DYNAMIC DELIGHT
OVER AESTHETIC PURITY
(2002)

WHAT'S NEW / MATERIAL FEEL
VERSUS ABSTRACTION

Lately I've been feeling an urge to change architecture. Or to put it more grandly, to create buildings that are not of the twentieth century.

Looking at the Matsumoto Performing Arts Centre, probably the biggest change is how little glass there is. People might think that's because it's a theatre. But no, in the initial competition design all external walls were glass; we only changed them to fibreglass-reinforced precast concrete (GRC) at the construction documentation stage, largely because of the immediate surroundings, but even before that we'd been discussing covering the glass surfaces with film or using some plainer material like aluminium panels.

Formerly, I was always thinking how to minimise the sense of materiality. I was stuck on 'pure', 'plain', 'abstract' surfaces – the very hallmark of Mies-style twentieth-century architecture, and further stressed by today's increasingly high-rise buildings. The concrete we used for the external walls in Matsumoto, however, is opaque. The panels are inlaid with handmade glass accents in seven different sizes, but still the effect is wholly unlike ordinary plate glass. This is something we developed together with a glass manufacturer: sandwiching a steel framework between two panels allows us to use the same material inside and out, with same-size glass accents aligned in matching positions. Since completion, we've seen a lot of people touching the inlaid glass; the rough texture of the handmade glass seems to invite hands.

Aside from these cement panels, we used several other textural materials: cast aluminium panels on the exterior of the flytower and small hall, wood-laminated corrugated steel panels in graduated tones from deep wine-red to light pink covering the large hall, and custom woven fabric for upholstering the theatre seating.

By not minimising the material qualities but instead exposing the materials outright, we sought an effect that is more textural than visual, something closer to Le Corbusier, say, than to Mies.

SPREADING RIPPLES / SEQUENCES

Seen from above, Matsumoto delineates a curious shape. People ask me if it's supposed to resemble some string instrument like a violin, but of course no such simple symbolism was ever intended. Rather, the image for these two 'antenna' halls was one of concentric circles spreading out like ripples until they came to fill the site. I'm never satisfied until the design lives up to the beautiful curves I imagined, so even though the site was quite big I wasn't about to switch to another programme for unifying the space. In other words, I didn't want to resort to any one straightforward scheme, axial alignment, grid system or whatever.

As with the tubes in the Sendai Mediatheque, random centre points generate radiating ripples, the interference of which serves to energise the space. Only in Matsumoto, the points are fewer, and the closed spaces of the halls prevented such an open rendering of the spatial concept.

Building typologies such as theatres and concert halls give renewed priority to acoustic and visual restrictions. The type of performance or concert determines the size and configuration of the stage; even with different audience capacities, it is not easy to break away from certain set formats. As building types, halls have carried over from

the nineteenth century into modern architecture.
Matsumoto is the third hall I've designed up to now
(following Nagaoka Lyric Hall and T Hall in Taisha), and
none of them has escaped the customary hall typology.
The Matsumoto Performing Arts Centre's large hall had
to accommodate traditional opera as well as ordinary
theatre productions, so we provided U-shaped audience
seating augmented with four levels of balconies on three
sides of the main stage. Likewise, with the 240-seat small
hall, the stepped banks of fixed seats plus galleries to either
side conform to traditional norms. The only part in which
we tried to realise a more contemporary theatre was the
entrance to the foyer area. In Matsumoto the approach from
the entrance to the two halls is considerably elongated;
the distance to the large hall is especially long because
the seating area is placed further away than the stage with
respect to the entrance. Moreover, there are steps up a
gentle incline from the entrance at ground level to the foyer
at a level some 6m higher up.

In addition to these extraordinarily large and elongated entrance foyer areas, there is on the roof a large
rehearsal room along with a garden, which I had wanted
to use for an open-air performance space as an alternative
to the closed halls. The entrance hall steps, a corner of
the foyer, the rooftop garden – any of these, I wanted to
propose, could be a performance space. Alternatively,
the GRC building shell could have been articulated with
various changing elements so as to soften the sequence
that theatre-goers might experience in moving from city
street to closed hall. These spaces would inform different
individual experiences – nothing like the overall unifor-
mity imposed by an axis or a grid. While the hall itself
might follow Western models, the introduction of amply
fluid spaces gives the overall architecture a completely
different character to both the classic Western theatre and
the modernist theatre. I simply wanted to create a freer
kind of theatre space.

TRANSPARENCY CUT OFF FROM NATURE

The dominant quality of twentieth-century architecture was, in a word, 'purity': an ideal of untainted, unadulterated singularity. Thus, 'pure architecture' in the twentieth century had a transparent, abstract, strictly geometric, functionalist image exemplified by, needless to say, the works of Mies van der Rohe and early Le Corbusier.

Among such works, 'transparent architecture' in particular continues to proliferate throughout the world to this day. The dream of living in a clear box high in the sky, first imagined by Mies in his 1922 Glass Skyscraper, has become reality as people have sought out ever higher, ever more transparent quarters over the last 80 years.

Now, humans as a species originally had to dwell near soil and water like other creatures. Despite this, they abandoned nature and flocked to the cities, enamoured of tall glazed office buildings and residential tower blocks; they became hooked on transparent spaces as if on drugs.

I once wrote an essay titled 'Architectural Scenery in the Saran Wrap City',[1] referring to what I saw in Tokyo as a sprawl of utterly neutral, deodorised, homogeneous buildings, all replicating in a city without time or place. The most prevalent example of this was the ubiquitous 'convenience store'.

Until only very recently we would drink well water or tap water without a second thought. Now, however, most city dwellers drink bottled water as if water in clear PET bottles removed from a natural context was more reassuringly pure. The same holds for fresh foods wrapped in Saran wrap. People used to be accustomed to selecting fresh vegetables, meat and fish by direct smell and touch – instinctive 'animal senses' – but we now seem to believe that the clear plastic seal guarantees freshness. Almost without exception, every fresh food item sold in convenience stores comes packaged in plastic, robbed of any real material qualities by a thin layer of film and transformed into an abstract symbol. Having grown used to repeatedly choosing visually appealing surrogate 'stuff' in colourless convenience stores that negate all smell and touch, we came to demand that vapid clarity not only in physical space and things, but also in people.

An example that should still be fresh in mind is the incident that occurred in Kobe in 1997. A then third year middle-school boy of 14 killed an elementary school student and sent very peculiar declarations of his crime to the newspapers, more than once decrying his own 'transparent existence':

Transparent entity that I am – both up to now and from here on as well – I've gone to all this trouble to get everyone's attention because I wanted society to at least recognise, if only in their imagination, that I exist.

The pseudo-education that created this transparent thing I am . . .

Just once, I wanted to talk things over with friends who embody the same transparent existence as myself.

Here too we see a Saran-wrapped body. As the boy so aptly points out, our contemporary society keeps pushing the city and individuals toward a blank quasi-existence, turning people into abstract entities. What price this so-called liberation from the impure body?

FROM ABSTRACTION TO SENDAI

The Sendai Mediatheque was an important turning point for me. At the competition stage, the proposed model still aspired in its transparency to a Mies-like pure abstraction. In his summary report the chair of the jury, Arata Isozaki, dubbed the proposal somewhat cynically 'an *otaku* media space' 'faced with cool, frosted virtual-feel surfaces of no more depth than what's behind a CRT screen', 'Ito's proposal is a spotless germ-free operating room where not a drop of blood ever spills, a vision of virtual transparency where strangers see each other almost as shadows.'

Granted, at the time, I myself had envisioned a place for computer *otaku* to encounter their electronic bodies, an ethereal space free of material qualities. I was rudely awakened from that dream by visiting the steel foundry where they were making the gigantic tube and slab elements for the construction. The sight of the workmen battling with all that steel hit me with such a strong material impact. Steelworkers had told me that 'steel is a living thing', which sounded like utter nonsense until I actually witnessed those masses of steel stretching and bending with heat: the raw dynamic of real material was much more appealing than any pure, abstract beauty – so much so that I began to wonder whether another kind of architecture might be possible, a total departure from the clear, pure 'less is more' model.

The Sendai Mediatheque as completed might appear cool and abstract as ever, but my real interest had shifted to the steel structure; my quest was now oriented toward spaces for the biophysical animal.

MATERIALS AND STRUCTURE /
THE CURSE OF TRANSPARENCY

After Sendai, my focus became 'living enjoyment over pure aesthetics'. But how to go about realising that objective?

For the time being I addressed that goal via questions of materials and structure. And, of course, the materials we developed for the Matsumoto Performing Arts Centre are one such exploration. More exciting, however, was the discovery that material issues do not stop at materials alone. The previously discussed opaque GRC walls, for instance, opened new vistas on long-standing notions about the division of interior and exterior.

In Sendai, my thinking had been to erase distinctions between inside and out by means of very light, thin, highly transparent membrane walls. And yet this fixation on lightness and thinness only served to cement barriers squarely before me because, as it turns out, the more abstract and dematerialised the architecture, the bigger the issues of demarcation become. Transparency is a trap, a fundamental contradiction inherent in Mies-style modernist architecture. Conversely, switching to very concrete materials such as the GRC panels in Matsumoto was liberating. Despite the newly developed material and very large enclosing wall, one somehow doesn't feel isolated from the surrounding environment. It made me keenly aware how much of a curse the pursuit of pure transparency had been. A slight shift in perspective suddenly resolved what had been an acute conundrum.

Likewise, material questions combined with structural issues to trigger major developments in my thinking. Though not yet fully realised in Matsumoto, the attempt to unify the shell material with the structure was a new direction that led to the Bruges Pavilion and the Serpentine Pavilion (both 2002) and the Tod's Omotesando Building (2004).

In Bruges, a planar structure system of aluminium honeycomb gives the pavilion its distinctive look. That is, while a honeycomb core alone would have been too weak for a bearing frame, affixing aluminium reinforcing panels in key places also creates decorative effects, with the open honeycomb areas visible between the aluminium ovals creating oval patterns. The size and spacing of the ovals seems altogether freehand – which it is. Structures can be put together out of ovals or circles or rectangles by means of planar configurations that also make for a 'happier' look. Utterly different from reductive modernist abstraction, here the abstraction is more flexible and inclusive.

The same can be said of the Serpentine Pavilion. An 18m cube supported solely by its square faces, it has no transversal grids: the structural articulation is instead achieved by rotating progressively smaller inset squares, so that weight from above is not distributed evenly out to the sides, but circulates outward via a more dynamic spatial kinaesthesia. Step inside the structure, and one hardly feels enclosed in a cube; the space seems simultaneously interior and exterior, as if all six faces could easily flip inside-out.

The Tod's Omotesando Building represents a combination of GRC panels from Matsumoto together with structural innovations from the Serpentine. The poured concrete structure provides its own decorative element, although the Serpentine's rotated square geometric pattern has been replaced by an overlapping tree pattern – geometric, but clearly different in character to a pure abstract geometry. Moreover, by making the surface and structural elements identical, we do away with that standard of twentieth-century architecture: curtain-wall construction. Thus, as with the Serpentine, we achieve a spatial equality between inside and out, while at the same time creating a facade that looks entirely different to the plainness of evenly articulated curtain-wall facades.

Modernist architecture is all too familiar to both architects and users alike. We'd convinced ourselves that plain, unadorned, transparent, abstract spaces were ultimate beauty. As if pure geometric forms like squares and round columns were the only possible geometries, or optimally functional combinations thereof were absolutely appropriate everywhere. That's how we designed buildings, and that's how we used them. Can't we by now have architecture based on different values? Isn't it time for buildings to offer 'dynamic delight over aesthetic purity'? Slowly but surely my conviction deepens with each new endeavour. All of which makes me want to change architecture.

NOTE

1. Published in *Gendaishiso*, September 1992, and reprinted in *Tousou suru Kenchiku* (Tokyo: Seidosha, 2000), 208–16.

THE NEW 'REAL':
TOWARD RECLAIMING MATERIALITY
IN CONTEMPORARY ARCHITECTURE
(2006)

June 2006 found me on the ground floor of the Neue Nationalgalerie in Berlin, standing atop a field of white mounds some 1,000m^2 in size whose undulating surface was crowded with a sea of people. On display were artworks created in response to these mounds by more than a dozen artists. Some had taken it as their unframed 'canvas' and spray-painted bright colours directly on the white ground; others bored holes in it, crawled inside and proceeded to paint murals that recalled cave paintings drawn by primitive humans; still others excavated hollows (something like capsule-hotel rooms or impromptu shelters devised by homeless persons) in which to install their work, demanding that visitors sit or lie down in order to appreciate it from below.

Naturally, not all artists elected to work in response to the mounds. There were those who wholly ignored them or simply hung their work on walls as usual. Nonetheless, the undulating floor surely did elicit different responses from the artists than the typical 'white cube' interior.

Why, then, did I design such mounds? Because I wanted to transform Mies's flat floor and soften the rigid near-perfection of his grid system.

Mies van der Rohe is considered the creator of the uniform grid that dominated twentieth-century architecture. Completed in 1968, the Neue Nationalgalerie is a work from the very last years of a life spent entirely in pursuit of grids, and indeed may be said to be the summation of his grid thinking. With its large flat roof floating above a raised base, its square plan encased in glass on all four sides, its symmetry of cruciform columns with its core element placed exactly in the centre – this is a temple, a paean to twentieth-century Euclidean geometry.

Yet the more total the grid system, the more perfect and pure the geometric space, the less I felt like putting up partition walls in accordance with that geometry. No, I wanted to dissolve its modular regularity, to transform its floor into rolling hills. Not to destroy Mies's space or oppose it, but simply to try to shift it into a different orientation – a nudge toward what I now call the 'emerging grid'. The architecture I now seek pushes Euclidean geometry in the direction of non-linear geometries based on nature, because I feel that people are losing their sensitivity and vitality within such pervasive grid-form urban environments and architectural spaces.

Uniform grid space characterises most cities today. New York, Chicago, Los Angeles, Toronto, Beijing, Shanghai, Singapore, Tokyo are all virtually indistinguishable inorganic continuums of glass and steel, utterly artificial environments bearing no relation to nature. Countless people work there, driven by the dictates of economics and information, their lives spent looking away from real material things as they fret and fritter their days in abstract boxes held by the abstract machinations of money.

Was the final aim of Mies's famous aphorism 'less is more' to have people live in a Cartesian vacuum? The vision of unemotional, never-sweating professionals gazing silently at computer monitors in spaces impossibly divorced from nature may well be the ultimate, most beautifully abstract goal of the twentieth century, yet beyond that what is there to see but the ruins of modernism devoid of even those cool-and-dry workaholics?

I began to want to show the material strength of such abstract, inorganic spaces only after the Sendai Mediatheque began construction. The building is simple in composition: 13 randomly placed 'tubes' made of steel pipes support seven layered square 'plates,' creating an empty interior penetrated by large tree trunk-like columns and enclosed by glass; each 'honeycomb panel' floor comprises a pair of 50m² steel sheets that sandwich polygonal ribbing, effectively eliminating the need for beams. The strong contrast between organic-shaped 'tubes' and thin, highly abstract 'plates' almost seems like planting a grove of trees across an otherwise manmade expanse. Or rather, it suddenly brings pure geometries into nature and sets them up in striking counterpoint, like a cube cut out of a forest-like continuum to fit the actual site and programmatic conditions – hence all the facades are simply lopped-off cross-sections.

Humans who once lived in the caves and forests of the natural world used to cut down trees to build shelters for themselves. Such shelters became 'architecture' only after they were given independent form and geometric order. Marc-Antoine Laugier describes the primitive hut as 'le modèle sur lequel on a imaginé toutes les magnificences de l'Architecture.'[1] I take this to mean that the essence of architecture since ancient times has been an independent formal order that stemmed from the natural world. Twentieth-century modernism replaced the order of round columns and pediments with an order of simple, abstract perpendicular lines. As we have already seen in the Neue Nationalgalerie, this order derived from a uniform grid totally independent from nature.

But we might just as easily say that the 'tubes' introduce a different geometry into an otherwise pure Cartesian coordinate grid, using gigantic steel members no less. Thus, both in Berlin and in Sendai, contrary to the historical order of architecture taking shape within nature, I attempted the reverse process: to induce nature out of built forms, as well as to inject materiality into 'less is more' space, precisely in order to return some living reality to the void of economics and data. We might call this a 'new real' in materiality beyond modernism. Not merely nostalgic or superficial touches, my challenge was to envision a whole new way of architecture.

In the endeavour to regain material power in architecture, structure offers important clues. Like the skeletal and muscular systems of the human body, structural members physically support buildings by directly transmitting loads. In past architecture, however, these essentially dynamic flows were sealed within the static geometries of formal architectural orders, as when Vitruvius likened balance in symmetrical stasis to the body circumscribed within circles and squares despite the dynamic equilibrium of the body in motion. Likewise, twentieth-century uniform grid architecture forced loads to flow along uniform perpendicular lines. Yet in either age, the dynamism of flowing forces remained concealed within classical geometric orders.

But computer technologies are now liberating architecture from Euclidean geometries. They are enabling the realisation of the unstable fluidity of the moving body and the complex balance of growing plant life in architectural space.

The structural engineers I have collaborated with since Sendai – Mutsuro Sasaki, Cecil Balmond, Masato Araya, Masahiro Ikeda – all possess a gift for structural analyses based in nonlinear mathematics. These people are creating structures out of the complex, dynamic interplay of forces – 'fluid body architectures' that would have been inconceivable, let alone attainable, last century. In Sasaki's designs for Grin Grin (Island City Central Park, Fukuoka) or the Crematorium in Kakamigahara, for instance, continuous spaces are realised within three-dimensionally curved free-form shells. In both these projects, he was readily able to analyse structures directly from the shape of virtually any curved surfaces we could imagine. Of course, he would first rely on his own intuition as a structural expert to tell him which shapes looked potentially viable, then coax and correct the forms in the proper direction. Yet even so, his approach is nothing like heretofore prevailing methods; up to now, before entering into simulations, the structural engineer would first establish conventional structural schema, analysis being possible only within those formats. In other words, no matter how freely the architect might imagine his forms, he would have to somehow fit them into the engineer's predetermined frameworks. With Sasaki's new methods, however, the available frameworks have so greatly expanded that the architect has all the freedom he could possibly want. As Sasaki explains:

However, taking the design as the given conditions, with the aim of obtaining it as the resulting structure, would be an original structural design procedure for creating a structure that conforms to the desired design while following mechanical principles. A process of directly finding the optimum structural type and shape that satisfies the design parameters of the desired space is called design analysis, or shape analysis. Utilising structural mechanics as an integrated design method, this process is completely opposite to the sequential approach of conventional structural analysis, and is therefore a kind of reverse analysis.[2]

The continuous shell in Island City is a good example of this reverse analysis. Here three shells with open centres alternate in a convex–concave sequence describing something like a spiral, a major departure from the conventional 'shell' typology. Studies for the three-part shell began with rendering a physical model, which was then measured in order to create digital data and ultimately produce a structural simulation. As a result, we can experience a highly dynamic topological space.

Araya's structural analysis for the Tod's Omotesando Building followed a similar process. Beginning with the image of overlapping tree silhouettes that was proposed by me as the architect, he proceeded to examine how the stresses would flow in such a complex network of crisscrossed branches. All the branching shapes were immediately digitised to create a simulation, which was then repeatedly amended and adjusted toward equilibrium along the chosen parameters; each partial change in the shape of a single branch would affect the equilibrium of all the other branches, hence the permutations were potentially limitless.

Araya's efforts at analysing complex stress flows would have been next to impossible a decade ago. Computer technology has revolutionised our ability to dissect structural forms – columns, beams, braces, walls.

The tree-shaped structural members in Tod's are symbolic in the sense that each tree yields its own equilibrium yet never repeats, a rich variation of forms that reflects the biodiversity of the natural world.

Cecil Balmond, the structural engineer with whom I collaborated on the Serpentine Pavilion 2002 in London's Hyde Park, is not just a technical whiz but, in his words, a 'natural philosopher'. He takes great interest in the auto-nomic shaping of the natural world, in how its component molecules behave and organise into various structures.

His conceptual approach to drawing a rectangle, for instance, does not seek a constant form but rather 'the energy of one line in relation to the energy of the other line', which he pursues as 'a ratio or frozen time constricting movements in space'.[3] Thus, to him, geometry always consists in the tracks of moving points: the application of certain parameters to the endless multiplicity of countless streaming points and the line traces they leave, rules governing directions and intersections that inform his concept of architectural structure. What up to now have been pure shapes – circles, squares and cubes – he has totally reconceived as selected frozen moments in the ongoing motions of points.

The surface of the Serpentine Pavilion, seemingly a random network of tangled lines, comprises a structure of flat steel bars formed according to Balmond's precise algorithms, which embed squares in rotating concentric succession, a dynamic twist that transforms the pure geometric shapes into a spiralling environment.

As the lines race over the plane, shooting down the sides at angles only to kick back through the base and rise up the other side, the surface becomes a mesh of circuits, going nowhere and yet at the same time moving towards

everywhere. Normal extension ceases; we are in a time capsule. We occupy space that undermines the idea of limit, denying skin to volume.[4]

For a fact, the experience of being inside the pavilion with no visible columns and beams or windows and doors, none of the usual hierarchy of architectural forms, is that of space itself – an ever-fluctuating, self-recursive abstract space whose interior and exterior are contiguous, not at all organic yet filled with a curious vitality.

Two as yet uncompleted projects, the Forum for Music, Dance and Visual Culture in Ghent and the Taichung Metropolitan Opera House, utilise similar structural systems to create maze-like continuums of three-dimensionally curved spaces, all very complex in appearance yet based on clear and simple principles.

Two parallel horizontal planes divided into uniform grids, each with alternating circles circumscribed in a chequerboard array, are positioned so that the circles above and below are one square out of congruity with each other; these circles are then interconnected as if via resilient membranes, the three-dimensionally curved surfaces of the 'membranes' dividing the floor plan into distinct spaces. By further stacking this system in a vertical direction, the articulated spaces form continuous vertical and horizontal 'tubes' respectively. If the grid and circles are kept uniform in size, then all tubular spaces would also be equal, but varying their sizes and shifting their centres yields a complex array of irregular spaces.

We have dubbed this the 'emerging grid': a system by which a uniform grid is manipulated to yield a continuum with a three-dimensionally curved shell; a method for transforming simple, regular spaces into complex ones rich in variation and the hard and inorganic into the supple.

During the Ghent competition, we experimented with numerous variations using this process, arriving at the requisite 1,800-seat concert hall, dance/orchestra rehearsal studios and rooms for workshops. But instead of a conventional auditorium, we proposed that the hall be an extension of the exterior urban space, so that the casual ease of outdoor concerts would carry over into the interior. Or to put it another way, we attempted a convoluted 'networking' of the street into the building, inserting spaces that could be used for music and dance performances. It was the 'emerging grid' system that allowed us to realise a volumetrically interconnected image of streets capable of satisfying all the preconditions.

The tubes that ran vertically in Sendai span the entire Ghent project horizontally and vertically. The space is continuous throughout, though, as at Sendai, the tubes are cut off to fit to the site, exposing cross-sections to the perimeter as curved waveforms – analogous to the arteries that run through the human body. Are the intestines and oesophagus internal or external organs? One might ask the same thing about the 'sound tubes' in Ghent. It is amazing to see how submitting a uniform grid to a series of algorithms can deliver such organic spatial qualities.

Likewise in Taichung, albeit carried further than in Ghent, the three theatre spaces required for opera and drama seemed to demand self-contained conventional spaces, yet by utilising the 'emerging grid' we were able to create spaces closer to caverns than tubes – and infused with energy.

In any case, surface network structural systems as in Tod's or the Serpentine Pavilion are now applied to three-dimensional surfaces in Grin Grin or Kakamigahara as total spatial network systems.

Most of the projects we have done since Sendai are very likely unrepeatable 'handmade' efforts. Reinforcing struts have been moulded to complex three-dimensionally curved surfaces, steel ribs and plates, requiring enormous numbers of precision welds and pieces of glass cut to different irregular shapes, which then had to be individually fitted into concrete frames – all incredibly demanding operations. The sheer amount of energy and exactitude invested in realising these 'problematic' buildings is testament to our aims to find a 'new real' material power in architecture.

The various specific projects we have looked at thus far all exemplify a common thesis that can be summed up as follows:

1. Liberate architecture from staid prevailing forms via dynamic stress flows.

2. Transform modernist 'less-is-more' minimal spaces into primal 'real places' in tune with nature.

Contemporary architecture – and especially Japanese contemporary architecture – is almost entirely concerned with modernist sophistication. Minimal and stoic, many buildings showcase a pure geometric beauty, but do they really invigorate people? In some ways, nothing spoils creative impulses as much as sophistication, as art history all too often shows.

In today's world, where buildings have been reduced to mere 'consumables' in the scheme of economics and information media, what we seek in architecture are spaces that are truly alive, that actually engage us physically. I could sum this up in two dictums: 'Fluid spaces in which we can feel the dynamic stress flows' and 'Nature-conscious spaces with primitive qualities akin to tree houses and caves'. Not that I advocate a return to the past: I'm staking the latest technologies on the 'new real' dream beyond modernism.

First published in *Toyo Ito: The New 'Real' in Architecture* (Tokyo: Tokyo Opera City Art Gallery, 2006)

NOTES

1. Marc-Antoine Laugier, *Essai sur l'architecture* (new edition 1755), 9.

2. Matsuro Sasaki, *Flux Structure*, translated by Thomas Daniell (Tokyo: Toto Shuppan, 2005), 49–51.

3. 'Cecil Balmond Meets Toyo Ito', *a+u* Issue 404 (May 2004), 46.

4. Cecil Balmond quoted in 'Serpentine Gallery Pavilion 2002: Toyo Ito with Arup', telescoweb.com.

LEARNING FROM A TREE
(2009)

The Tokyo Aoyama Hospital, which was located adjacent to my office, has been demolished. Having stood for close to 40 years, a building that still served its purpose was tragically smashed to pieces, and it pained my heart to see it turning into a mountain of rubble as the days passed.

While it was being demolished, I gathered three young architects to initiate a fictitious project, intended for publication. Gazing from a nearby vantage point at this moribund building being attacked by power shovels, they were inspired to conceive some kind of architecture for the cleared land, located between Shibuya Station and Omotesando Avenue, just off Aoyama Avenue. Bordered by wood-framed houses, small apartment blocks and office buildings, the site is also surrounded by larger facilities such as expensive high-rise condominiums and the United Nations University. The site of the demolished hospital (about 18,000m²) has probably been sold to a major developer, and will be reborn as high-rise condominiums, offices or commercial establishments. In central Tokyo, residential districts are constantly being redeveloped as high-rise buildings without logical connections to their surroundings.

Confronted with urban spaces undergoing constant dynamic transfigurations in accordance with the principles of the market economy, while having almost no chance to design anything but the smallest buildings, it was natural for these young architects to want to inscribe their own dreams on this vast piece of land. Their point of departure was surely the unbearable thought of this architecture being cruelly destroyed, and the feeling of regret at being able to do no more than watch the characterless redevelopment that will probably replace it. These three people, each in their own way, have been frustrated by urban development that prioritises economics, but they have not given up on the possibility of enriching Tokyo.

Whether building condominiums or offices, the method undertaken by major developers today is to calculate the vertical extent of the architecture and produce green spaces and public areas at ground level. This can be described as an emulation of the type of urban planning advocated by Le Corbusier in the first half of the twentieth century, through his Contemporary City for Three Million People and Plan Voisin for Paris. However, in a situation of fragmented private land-ownership such as the residential districts of Tokyo, the areas for redevelopment are naturally limited and, in many cases, adjacent to groups of low-rise homes. The imbalance of high-rise buildings suddenly projecting from groups of low-rise homes constantly appears in central Tokyo.

Why isn't the high-rise architecture more continuous with these groups of low-rise homes? Rather than huge, vertical boxes, why not architecture with multiple pleats that allow sufficient light, air and water to permeate the interiors? That is to say, can we not depict high-rises as dense, complex life forms that are deeply influenced by the natural environment? We started our project with the desire to visualise such a concept. While this may appear unrealistic, it might also be thought of as the first step toward magnificent urban and architectural images for the twenty-first century. In a world where economics is given priority over everything else, we architects must attempt to depict grand visions that respond to the question 'Where should we live tomorrow?'

Everyone is talking about architecture that is sympathetic to the global environment, ecological, sustainable and so on, but rather than being open to the natural environment most of what is being built now is oriented toward reinforcing inside/outside boundaries, constructing stable artificial environments, and installing devices such as solar cells. For human beings, who want to sense nature essentially as if they were a part of nature, like animals, this is a complete reversal of priorities.

We Asians live in cities that have integrated nature and architecture. Even just looking at the old maps and *byobu* (folding screen) pictures of Edo, we can read the ways in which arrays of villages are skilfully woven into the terrain and water flows. Our task is to take the densities of these pleated, fractal urban spaces and raise them to the level of high-rise buildings.

Looking directly at the reality before them and then beginning to think concretely and conceptually, the three young architects all had the desire to depict 'architecture like a tree that spreads its branches widely'. In continuity with the surrounding groups of low-level buildings and ground-level trees, the initial image was an inverted pyramidal form that becomes broader as it rises toward the centre. As the image developed further – the ground level being left as an open space like a public park, with a complex, arboreal space extending its leaves and branches above it – the architecture increasingly came to resemble a huge camphor tree. However, this resemblance extends beyond the form to the behaviour of a tree that has sprouted and grown to maturity.

What kind of architecture is like a large tree? We observed large trees and listened to lectures by tree experts. What became clear during our research was the highly interesting and unexpected essence of trees. We had thought that a tree growing in a certain environment was delicately, deeply interlinked with the surrounding vegetation. We also thought that trees and shrubs coexisted in intimate relationships so as to increase their longevity. Certainly, trees relate to each other, but according to the experts, these relationships are apparently only epiphe-nomenonal. That is to say, each tree egotistically insists on its presence so as to maintain its dominance over the others, and a delicate, dynamic balance is established through such reciprocal battles. Is it not true to say that such relationships are extremely similar to the mutual relationships between nations, corporations and people in a capitalist society?

When conceiving architecture, we architects tend to think about finalised, idealised images. To the degree that the surrounding environment is disordered, we try to make plans that form an independent order unrelated to their context. But in the natural world, if a tree tried to implement such an independent, idealised image, it would be destroyed in an instant. However egotistically it might attempt to live, a tree can only survive within a vast number of relationships.

We may consider this fact an important lesson for thinking about contemporary architecture. There are many messages we can learn from a tree. For instance, the approximate shape of a tree is set by its DNA, but each individual case is determined according to its interrelations with the surrounding environment as it grows. Led to its own most advantageous conditions, it flexibly interacts with the environment through incessantly repeated feedback. Even though the total image may have been set from the outset, this does not mean that its growth is closed with regard to the environment; on the contrary, it remains extremely open. Furthermore, while repeating a simple branching rule, a tree sustains a truly complex and diverse order. The large, thick branches near the ground have infinite potential to thinly and delicately divide in proportion to their closeness to the apex. In other words, it is endowed with a fractal shape. Extending vertically and horizontally to receive as much sunlight as possible, it vigorously tries to photosynthesise. In this way, the iterative unevenness of the entire outer layer blurs the concepts of inside/outside and front/back. Despite providing a strong sense of shelter, there is no sense of an inside/outside boundary below a large tree.

These diverse properties with which a tree is endowed are all important themes that should be referred to when we conceive architecture today. As architectural themes, they can be described and arranged as follows.

1. Thinking about architecture must be based on relativistic relationships with the environment.

2. The overall image of a work of architecture should not be unequivocally decided, but begin with a loose image that is gradually clarified by repeating various simulations.

3. While based on simple rules (geometry), architecture should be composed with a complex order.

4. By means of fractal geometry, the outer surface of architecture should produce ambiguous inside/outside boundaries.

5. Architecture must be open to the environment.

All of these are antagonistic to the themes of twentieth-century modernist architecture. The principles of modernist architecture – independence from nature, a pursuit of functionalism based on pure, lucid geometries – dominate the world even now, but we may at last escape this dominance and acquire the confidence to conceive architecture based on entirely new principles. For the supple sensitivities and bodily sensations of human beings to escape the paralysing spell of homogeneous spaces and restore a vivid and rich humanity, there are many things we can learn from a tree.

INSTEAD OF AN AFTERWORD
(2011)

Exactly 40 years have passed since I founded my own office. I can always identify several critical points in the process of designing a single project, and in a similar way there were points during this 40-year span that have determined the ideas influencing my architecture. Looking back, I feel that three important periods have greatly affected my thinking as an architect.

1. LOST DREAMS OF FUTURE CITIES (1971)

It was the middle of March when I established a first-class licensed architect's office on the fourth floor of a small building in Minami-Aoyama, Tokyo. Although this was the official founding of my design practice, nothing much changed from the previous two years I had spent on my own after resigning from Kiyonori Kikutake's office. I quietly continued doing only two or three jobs per year, though this meant that I didn't need to do much business management. My prospects of work extended no more than a few months ahead, a situation that continued for the next ten years, so thinking back now it was a miracle that I was able to keep two or three staff members employed. However, in a sense, my life had acquired a certain refinement. I relaxed at the drafting board all day, with *enka* [traditional Japanese ballad] records always spinning beside me. The singer I listened to the most was Shin'ichi Mori, and I felt that the metallic vibrato of his voice had a mysterious accord with the purified atmosphere of the city at that time.

My sole reason for naming the office 'Urban Robot'

was the ongoing influence of technology. Architects in the 1960s used it as the basis for depicting all manner of visionary urban dreams. This was exemplified by projects from Archigram and the metabolists. In particular, the brightest and most optimistic technological futures were depicted in the Archigram drawings of Instant City, Plug-in City and Walking City. But when Expo 70 was held in Osaka, I developed an instant distrust of technology.

The Aluminium House, my first work of architecture since becoming independent, was completed right at this period. So this house comprises a mixture of my tenacious dreams of technology and the new direction I had chosen: a more poetic yearning for a space of light. The house is characterised by two tubes of light, but the initial plan included four tubes, one for each member of the client's family. An information terminal and an energy terminal were to be installed below each tube. In other words, the premise was a spacesuit-like capsule that enabled each person to survive in the city.

Minoru Ueda, editor-in-chief of *Toshi Jūtaku* – the most fashionable and popular magazine at the time – published the Aluminium House and several other projects under the general heading of URBOT. The Aluminium House was a belated capsule project, but rather than people playing with machines, as depicted by the metabolists and Archigram, the people themselves were urban robots. In other words, despite depicting an apparatus for survival in the city, this was not a paean to a glittering technological future. It was an expression of the feeling of emptiness engendered by an unavoidable recognition of the fact that real urban spaces were beginning to be engulfed by an environment dominated by technology. Within this were isolated, autistic robots playing with light.[1]

My admiration for the visions of magnificent 'future cities' depicted by a group of young architects known as the metabolists, with Kenzo Tange at their head, inspired me to become an architect.

However, in the latter half of the 1960s, following the peak of 1964 Tokyo Olympics, those dreams suddenly collapsed. The Japanese economy at that time was booming, just as China's is now. Various schemes were implemented in order to flaunt this economic success. This was surely epitomised by the Osaka Expo 70. But the significance of these dreams lay precisely in the fact that they remained unfulfilled. The act of replacing reality with a dream became no more than an opportunity to celebrate our national pride.

Further influenced by the university protests of the late 1960s and the oil crisis of the early 1970s, Japan crossed the threshold of 1970 to enter an era of introversion, undergoing an inevitable change in direction. Faced with a stagnant economy, architects were no longer able to expect the nation to support their existence.

The two leading architects of the introverted architectural world of the 1970s were Arata Isozaki and Kazuo Shinohara. Sensitive to the mood of the era, Arata Isozaki promptly grasped the changing situation and announced, 'there is no future in architecture'. His verdict was that utopias now only existed in the minds of individuals. Isozaki was one by one introducing to Japan one-by-one the discourses of the most radical architects in the world at that time, among them Archigram, Hans Hollein, Superstudio and Charles Moore. 'Radical' means that they saw architecture as something not to be 'built', but rather 'demolished'. In 1975, a series of Isozaki's essays that had been published in an art magazine were collected into a book with the title *Kenchiku no kaitai* (*The Demolition of Architecture*). Needless to say, having been let down by the dream-like proposals for future cities, my generation was enthralled by the ideas of the radicals. My generation of architects – Tadao Ando, Itsuko Hasegawa, Kazunari Sakamoto, Osamu Ishiyama – had begun to design around the age of 30, but none of us were doing great work. We were instead just sitting around all day feeling gloomy.

Architecture is not something 'creative' but 'destructive'; 'architects should be critical toward real society' – after hearing phrases like that, our generation, known as the 'demolition generation', couldn't help but think of architecture as a type of critical statement.

Kazuo Shinohara, another leading figure, appeared in the 1960s as an aloof creator of houses. From the outset, he had no interest in the future city. Or perhaps it would be better to say that, through the publication of a succession of small, highly autonomous houses, he attempted to directly antagonise Kenzo Tange and the metabolists.

His House in White, published in 1967, had a particularly large impact on me. The tile-covered square roof set on a white-walled exterior evoked the traditional Japanese *minka* [vernacular house] but the internal spaces had an almost unbelievable freshness. With a single pillar located at the centre, the plan was divided into two spaces. It was just bisected by a single line, set slightly off-centre. The wider part was a double-height hall, and the narrower part a two-storey bedroom and kitchen. Consisting of only the three elements of the square plan, single pillar and single dividing line, this space had been distilled to a breathtaking degree. It was an 'abstract' space from which all impurities had been erased. However small it might have been, it condensed a degree of tension that was sufficient to defy the futuristic city schemes, and was infused with a strong critique of contemporary society.

It could be argued that the harsh messages presented by these two leaders of the 1970s – the architecture of demolition that turns its back on the city, and the miniature utopias suffused with criticism – constructed an identity for contemporary Japanese architecture that extends right up to the present day. Traditionally, the Japanese are skilled at making abstract spaces by eliminating many elements. Accordingly, it might be said that the contemporary meanings given to the 'abstract small house' by Kazuo Shinohara have traversed my generation and been inherited by young architects today. However, this 'abstraction' appears to shine most brightly when attached to a discourse of 'criticism' with regard to society. Arata Isozaki's message – his manifesto that 'there is no future in architecture' –

was materialised as an 'abstracted' of architecture that came to be replicated in architecture throughout the world. But at the same time, these works were burdened by the mutually exclusive dichotomy of becoming alienated from Japanese society. For me personally, and for the Japanese architectural world, 1970 was a time of great significance.

2. THERE IS NO NEW ARCHITECTURE THAT IS NOT IMMERSED IN THE SEA OF CONSUMPTION (1989)

I have long been aware that I frequently use the word 'city' when discussing my own architecture. Moreover, this word can usually be replaced with 'Tokyo'. Accordingly, even when I say 'city' my intention is not to connect my own architecture with the context of the physical city. It refers to the 'city' as the source of inspiration for my images of architectural space.

In this sense, 'Tokyo' in the latter half of the 1980s was for me a treasury of images. It was a city without precedent anywhere in the world: never, in my view, had a city been so disembodied in its economy and in its urban spaces. Most of the denizens of this city probably felt that the things they saw around them were illusory, and their traces would surely vanish like a dream at dawn; but on the other hand, perhaps one cannot enter a fleeting dream without becoming intoxicated.

I myself was like that. I couldn't help savouring the intoxicating sensation of my own body melting into spaces saturated with neon lights and consumer goods that one by one appeared and then disappeared. These spaces possessed a transparency and a density not found in the cities of the United States, even though they might seem like equally consumerist cultures.

Though I describe them as dense, these spaces had almost no reality as objects. In a state of near-stupefaction, I was sucked into these immaterial yet dense spaces for moments of glorious intoxication. This was the apotheosis of 'Tokyo'. So it could be said that the imagery of my architecture up to now has emerged from this 'Tokyo' apotheosis. The Pao for the Tokyo Nomad Girl dates from 1985, but it symbolically represents the relationship between my architecture and the consumerist city. That is to say, it manifests a critical view toward lifestyles that are fully immersed in the spaces of consumption, but at the same time it cannot conceal my own attraction to the freedom and freshness offered by such lifestyles.

In periods like the present day, wherein one cannot gain an overview of society as it undergoes complex, diverse transformations, the difficulty of building architecture lies in the way one perceives its distance from reality. It no longer seems possible to loudly proclaim the validity of early twentieth-century modernism. The architecture of today is predicated on a denial of reality, and moreover, rather than the pursuit of innovative proposals, its far-and-away most important role seems to be the lucid spatialisation of single, apparently simple aspects extracted from our existing complex reality. In other words, the distance between such architectural proposals and real society is vanishingly small. But it seems that the energy from which architecture is created today lies precisely in this infinitesimal difference.[2]

Entering the 1980s, the stagnant Japanese economy began to display vigour once more. This reached a peak in the latter half of the decade, with the so-called bubble. Tokyo above all was fiercely prosperous, just as I depicted it above.

With the sudden increase of land prices in Tokyo, bizarrely, the cost of high-quality architecture paled in comparison to the cost of the land. So land speculation enabled the demolition of buildings that had been constructed and never even used. My restaurant-bar 'Nomad' was demolished less than two years after its completion. From the moment the design was commissioned, it was decreed to be a temporary architecture with a maximum life of one or two years, so I wasn't surprised, but my feeling of emptiness was undeniable.

In the city centre during this period, small commercial buildings were being rebuilt with bewildering speed. Even if this could be justified in terms of investment, the pace was abnormal. The accelerating speed of rebuilding was undoubtedly related to a Japan-specific ethos of impermanence, in which a building may be rebuilt as long as the land is maintained.

During this time, the identity of contemporary Japanese architecture was further strengthened by, I think, the 'fictionality' of architecture. There was a proliferation of architecture valued for the meaning of its surfaces, but not as a physical object. We could have just called this 'empty architecture' and left it at that, yet if we instead dared to pursue the reality of that era by means of fictional urban spaces, this would not be regarded as a denial of the era or society, but as an attempt to invest architecture with the sense of corporeality that was being engendered by the era. Put another way, this would result in architecture suffused with an unprecedented degree of lightness and transparency.

By adding the 'fiction' of the 1980s to the 'abstract' and 'critical' architecture built in the 1970s, the 'abstraction' and 'criticality' became further radicalised.

3. SENDAI MEDIATHEQUE UNDER CONSTRUCTION (2000)

The construction of the Sendai Mediatheque has reached the final phase. No matter how often I visited the site, I would see only steel, but recently things have begun to change rapidly. The pipe columns, which I call 'tubes', are being covered with fireproof coating and fireproof paint, and many of them have begun to be clad with glass. The suspended ceiling is being hung below the steel plate floor slabs, on which raw welding marks are visible. The glazing of the exterior walls is being finished at last, and the internal partitions are being installed at the same time...

Perhaps one reason is that the architecture being erected is very different from the proposal made for the competition. The 'tubes' shown in the competition model certainly appeared to be rarefied structures with a gentle presence. The slabs called 'plates' also appeared to be obsessively thin, abstract sheets. However, the structure being assembled on site is completely different from this initial image. The 'tubes' and 'plates' are nothing more than raw steel. It is like seeing a huge steel sculpture being assembled, because of the 25mm-thick steel plate and 30mm-diameter steel pipe being welded around the 'tubes'. Not to mention that the process has a violent appearance far removed from conventional images of high-tech architecture. There are endlessly unfurling scenes of rust flakes swirling and sparks flying. Naturally, many people visited the site with preconceptions of a transparent, abstract architecture and they have been surprised at the huge discrepancies...

Perhaps the mystery of these spaces is not merely a question of spatial experience but has something to do with the way this architecture will be used. There is no one-to-one relationship of space and function, of this room being used for that purpose. A general usage has been assigned to each floor, but otherwise there are no regulations. This fact was a problem during the judging of the competition. Faced with the unprecedented architectural model (archetype) of the mediatheque, which provides spaces that may be used for anything, some felt that the actual proposal was just being postponed.

Over the ensuing five years, many people participated in frequent debates about what a mediatheque is, how should it be used, and so on. These debates still continue, even though it is only one year until the opening. In a sense, the construction process of this building might be called 'another mediatheque', and this other mediatheque is already in use. Put conversely, the completion of the mediatheque is not just the completion of the physical building as its hardware, and debates over the mediatheque are sure to continue even

after its completion. On this point, for the present, the mediatheque still might be called incomplete...

In this sense, the spaces we have constructed for the Sendai Mediatheque might yet again postpone the architectural model of a 'mediatheque'. However, it is precisely this postponement – in other words, precisely this state of being eternally 'under construction' – that is for me perhaps the most significant aspect of this architecture. Architecture without an 'archetype' is for me 'ideal architecture'.[3]

My architectural life was greatly altered by my experiences with the Sendai Mediatheque, from design through to construction. I don't mean this in terms of wider coverage in the media or an increasing number of commissions. To put it slightly grandiosely, this was an event large enough to transform my notion of architecture. It was the first time I was able to comprehend the architect as a presence in a society.

Since starting my atelier in 1971, to the degree that my own sense of beauty has been honed and my architectural thought has been radicalised, I have been progressively expelled from society, unavoidably becoming an architect who critiques society from the outside. So in the mediatheque competition proposal, I concentrated on obsessive beauty, obsessive abstraction and obsessive emptiness (one might even say blankness). In the judges' comments, Arata Isozaki – the head of the competition jury – gave my proposal the strange name 'architecture for the bodies of media *otaku*':

It achieves the purity of a sterile room. Or perhaps an operating theatre in which red blood has never been spilled. All the people one encounters are virtually transparent, in scenes that look just like silhouettes. This is what we can see on the other side of the cathode-ray tube, but manifesting it in a space that we can enter may well be appropriate for the architectural type of a mediatheque.

That was a pertinent comment on the competition proposal. But the architecture changed through the five-and-a-half year process, along with my own views on architecture.

My architecture lost its abstract beauty, and instead gained a more realistic strength. While the resulting qualities will be evaluated differently by each person, for the first time in my architectural life I had the feeling of 'being embraced by society'.

THINKING ABOUT ARCHITECTURE
FOR THE FUTURE

It goes without saying that I want to continue designing splendid architecture. But for a long time, I have had a dream of raising splendid young architects. More objectively than in my relationships with my own staff, but not within existing organisations such as universities, I want to encourage young people to think comprehensively about architecture.

Just as I was contemplating all this, I was given the chance to realise my own architectural museum (Toyo Ito Architecture Museum) on a small island in the Seto Inland Sea (Imabari City, Omishima). I decided to use the opportunity to inaugurate a small architectural school (Ito Architecture Institute) that will connect the island with Tokyo. It is scheduled to open in the summer of 2011.

What I want to achieve with the Ito Institute is not just to educate young architects but to be able to brainstorm with young people about architecture for the future – which boils down to 'thinking about architectural principles for the twenty-first century'.

As a result of taking the 'machine' as a model, the architectural principles of modernism tend to over-emphasise functionality and efficiency. An overzealous pursuit of scientific clarity has led to a severing of relationships with nature and a proliferation of artificial environments. Industrialised mass production enabled by technological progress may have been a success, but the world's cityscapes have become homogeneous. People all over the world may be shouting about saving energy, but most of their proposals depend on technology. If we continue to take the machine as our sole model, relying exclusively on technology, we will never reach fundamental solutions. Perhaps we should instead pursue architectural principles that enable reconciliation between nature and architecture, like premodern Japanese architecture. Cutting-edge technology should not be used to pursue clarity, but to create ambiguous boundaries between inside and outside.

I want to approach the task of constructing these new architectural principles at an extremely practical and unsophisticated level. It seems to me that modernist principles will never be transcended as long as we refuse to grasp architecture from the most primitive standpoints of 'For whom is architecture made?', 'Why is architecture made?' and 'How is architecture made?'

When visiting university studios or student diploma juries, I'm forced to listen to architectural concepts until I can't stand it any more, but these are no more than concepts made by architects for architects. However much students may talk about communities or methods of mass housing, most of them have zero consideration for human beings. While they depict innumerable people in their drawings and models, these are no more than abstractions of people. An architect located outside society can only advocate architectural principles from outside society.

I have been faced with this contradiction throughout the last 40 years. I now fervently wish to construct architectural principles that may be discussed from within society.

NOTES

1. *Kaze no henyoutai* (Tokyo: Seidosha, 2000), 10–14.
2. *Tousou suru architecture* (Tokyo: Seidosha, 2000), 12–14.
3. Ibid, 532–38.

Architecture Words 8
Tarzans In The Media Forest
Toyo Ito

All translations by Thomas Daniell, except:
'Garden of Microchips' translated by Hiroshi Watanabe
'Tarzans in the Media Forest' translated by
Shigeko Suzuki / Graham Thomson
'Dynamic Delight over Aesthetic Purity' and
'The New Real' translated by Alfred Birnbaum

Series Editor: Brett Steele

AA Managing Editor: Thomas Weaver
AA Publications Editor: Pamela Johnston
AA Art Director: Zak Kyes
Design: Wayne Daly
Editorial Assistant: Clare Barrett

Set in P22 Underground Pro and Palatino
Printed in Belgium by Die Keure

ISBN 978-1-902902-90-6

For a catalogue of AA Publications visit
aaschool.ac.uk/publications
or email publications@aaschool.ac.uk

AA Publications
36 Bedford Square
London WC1B 3ES
T + 44 (0)20 7887 4021
F + 44 (0)20 7414 0783

Supported by
the Great Britain
Sasakawa Foundation

The Great Britain
SASAKAWA
FOUNDATION